1999

The Great
City Academy Fraud

FRANCIS BECKETT

continuum

Continuum International Publishing Group
The Tower Building, 11 York Road, London SE1 7NX
80 Maiden Lane, Suite 704, New York NY 10038

www.continuumbooks.com

First published 2007

British Library Cataloguing-in-Publication Data
A catalogue record for this book is available from the British Library.

ISBN: 0–8264–9513–3 (hardback)

Typeset by Kenneth Burnley, Wirral, Cheshire
Printed and bound in Great Britain by Cromwell Press,
Trowbridge, Wiltshire

Contents

Acknowledgements

My first debt is to the National Union of Teachers and its General Secretary Steve Sinnott, without whose support, both financial and in terms of information, this book might not have been written.

John Bangs, head of its privatization unit, together with his colleagues Janet Theakston and Lucy Cavendish, have been key sources of information for me over several years. They have helped and advised me, and allowed me to make free with their copious research files.

None of this means that my conclusions are necessarily those of the NUT. The union has been punctilious in insisting that this is my book, and did not want to comment on its judgements, or try to influence them.

Local NUT representatives have given me a great deal of help, and I especially want to thank Ken Muller in Islington, Nick Grant in west London, Hank Roberts in Brent, and Ray Sirotkin in Lambeth.

Several fellow journalists have given generously of their information, time and contacts, in particular freelancers Fiona Millar, Mark Smulian and Wendy Wallace, and Linda Piper of the *Bromley News Shopper*.

I am grateful to several teachers who have talked to me, and two in particular: Gordon Potter, formerly deputy head teacher at Coulby Newham School, Middlesbrough, and Dr Gill Read, former senior teacher at Willesden High School. Without them

I would not have understood the full dishonesty of Government claims that academies were replacing failing schools.

As always, Margaret Tulloch, secretary of Comprehensive Futures, has been a source of information, ideas and wisdom.

I want to thank two of the many editors I have written for over the years. Throughout the seven years Peter Wilby was editor of the *New Statesman*, I wrote regularly for him about education. With his trust and encouragement I produced the education journalism I'm most proud of, including a series of pieces on city academies. And many years ago, in the early 1990s, Stephen Bates, then the *Guardian*'s education editor, asked me to write an obsequy over the grave of the Conservatives' city technology colleges. Without these two editors I might never have realized what dreadful scams these schemes are.

I also want to thank, for help, advice and contacts, Peter Lampl of the Sutton Trust, Paul Mackney of the University and College Union, and Christine Lewis of Unison. I've also benefited greatly from the help and enthusiasm of my editor at Continuum, Alexandra Webster.

Some academy sponsors and heads have given me interviews, knowing that I counted as a sceptic at best, and I want to record my thanks to them. I hope they feel that, while I have not always accepted the views they offered, I have presented them fairly. I particularly want to thank Lynn Gadd, principal of the Harefield Academy; Steve Chalke, chief executive of the Oasis Trust; Alastair Falk, former head of West London Academy and now chief executive of the Academy for Enterprise; and Lesley King, director of Academies Networks at the Specialist Schools and Academies Trust. Nigel McQuoid of the Emmanuel Schools Trust, as recorded in Chapter 5, has talked to me in the past, but this time agreed only to a useful off-the-record chat.

A couple of others talked to me on condition their names were not mentioned, and my sincere thanks go to them too.

No thanks at all to the politician at the centre of it all, Lord Adonis, who could not find time to talk to me, or even to answer a few emailed questions. It is more comfortable for a politician to talk only to those who agree with them, but someone should tell Lord Adonis that dissent is a key part of democracy. He might understand it himself if he had had to stand in an election, rather than owing his position entirely to Prime Ministerial patronage.

Introduction

If ever there was a Government policy characterized by political spin rather than substantiated evidence, it is the academies programme. The National Union of Teachers' campaigning document against academies has as its sub-title, *Looking Beyond the Spin*, to illustrate the need for an honest appraisal of this expensive and high-profile policy which impacts not just on the education of pupils in academies themselves, but on other neighbouring schools, and indeed on the whole publicly funded education system.

'A good local school for every child' is an aim shared by the majority of parents, governors, teachers and other education professionals. The 'independent' status of academies, which receive large amounts of capital funding and are governed and influenced by sponsors accountable to no one, is incompatible with this aim.

Ensuring that youngsters from the toughest backgrounds get a great start in life through educational opportunities has been at the heart of the National Union of Teachers' policies since it was founded. The issue is still with us. The academy initiative, however, is at best an expensive distraction from what has to be a priority for all those committed to ensuring that our education service meets the needs of all children.

Academies are an example of the marketization of education which has been embraced and promoted enthusiastically by this Government. Yet, when unpacked, the factors for success which the Government's evaluators of academies identify are no different from those characteristic of other successful schools: schools which are in receipt of markedly less capital funding and none of the hype of sponsor involvement.

The trade-off for this initiative comes at a high cost, however: over-expensive and often inappropriate buildings; high staff turnover; unrealistic expectations and a damaging effect on pupil admissions in surrounding schools. And, despite this, there are a number of academies which are facing difficulties. That some schools are in this situation is not a cause for celebration but a trigger for reflection by education policy-makers, the Government and all with a keen interest in our schools, on whether academy status is the best way of helping schools in the toughest and most socially deprived communities.

I am delighted to be able to commend Francis Beckett's book, *The Great City Academy Fraud*, to readers, while not agreeing with all his analysis, as a much-needed contribution to the debate on academies. Francis has turned a penetrating spotlight on various aspects of the academies programme. He looks at the origins of the initiative, the politics of its implementation, the rather murky world of the links between sponsors and political honours, and the disturbing evidence of the religious agendas of some of the academies' sponsors. This courageous publication provides an examination of the sub-text to the academies story, revealing the level of threat, promise and double-dealing which has gone on to enable the academies programme to get off the ground.

Francis brings out, in his chapter 'Sponsors in Ermine', the rather murky side of the academies programme. But, if there is a real scandal to be told, I fear that in the future it is likely to relate to handing over to rich sponsors powers over what and how children learn in a large number of schools.

This book should make disturbing reading for the Government, but it will certainly disturb parents and teachers even more. The chapter entitled 'How They Tore Up the Laws on Schools' shows how parents' objections to academies have been ignored and how pupils' and parents' democratic and human rights are being undermined by academies' 'independent' status; a situation which will only get worse as more academies open. This book provides the opportunity for the voices of those parents and pupils to be heard, with stories of unfair treatment jeopardizing young people's futures, which will give all but the most prejudiced supporter of academies pause for thought.

For the National Union of Teachers, a real strength of this book is the focus it gives to the experiences of those teachers who have spent their professional lives working in and with schools in the most challenging circumstances, who might have expected to have received some appreciation for their commitment and dedication. Unfortunately the academies programme has proved to be a tragedy in human terms for too many of these teachers.

The Government's political imperative of getting academies up and running and making progress has been achieved by denigrating many of the hard-won achievements of teachers and pupils in academies' predecessor schools. To date, no academy has replaced a school designated by Ofsted as requiring 'special measures'; indeed, many were recognized by Ofsted as doing a good job in very difficult circumstances. But these facts are incompatible with the Government's spin on how academy status and sponsor involvement has created a 'lift-off' effect. The teachers' voices in this book – many of them, I am proud to say, NUT members – give the lie to that myth: academy status in itself offers no magic solution. Indeed, there is none. This book shows that academy status can be deeply damaging to schools battling against the odds, and I commend it to you.

Steve Sinnott
General Secretary, National Union of Teachers

1

From Colleges to Academies

It all looked so hopeful in 1997. We had a new Government under a Prime Minister who told us that his priorities were 'Education, education, education.' Failing inner-city schools were at last to be given the money and the opportunity to start again.

Ten years after Tony Blair made us that promise, we are looking at the wreckage of a failed and discredited policy. How could something so obviously right have gone so horribly wrong? Why has a policy designed to make a better society become a byword for sleaze and political double-talk? How could we have ended up closing some good and tolerant schools, and often replacing them with bad and bigoted ones? How could the policy have become a weapon with which to trash the lives and careers of some of Britain's best and most dedicated teachers? And is there a darker purpose to it all?

This book is an attempt to answer these questions.

City academies, their sponsors and their principals, feel misunderstood and misused. 'The media is always very suspicious – there have been a lot of intemperate criticisms of academies' says Lesley King of the Specialist Schools and Academies Trust, the quango that promotes them. They feel they are doing their best to do good, and getting only brickbats in return. Most of them are there because they understand that education is the route out of poverty. They think children have been let down by bad and under-resourced schools, and they want to be part of a national movement which will change all that. They do not think the academy model is perfect, but it is the one the politicians have offered. The politicians tell them that anyone who opposes academies must also oppose having better schools for poor children. And they blame the messengers – the commentators like me – who tell them that the model has fatal design faults. But it is the politicians who have defrauded and betrayed them.

To understand what happened, we need to go back to October 1986, when the then Conservative Education Secretary, Kenneth Baker, announced the creation of a 'pilot network of 20 city technology colleges (CTCs) in urban areas' and appealed for 'potential sponsors in the business community, the churches and existing educational trusts'. Sponsors would own their CTCs, and run them, employing all staff. The Government would pay all running costs, but sponsors would contribute to the initial capital required to set them up.

If we look at the above brief sketch of the CTC idea from our vantage point two decades later, one thing screams out at us. These details are exactly the same as those of the city academy idea. In all essentials, city academies are the same as CTCs. So when the Labour Government arrived in 1997, it should have been able to look at the history of CTCs to see if the idea worked.

Here is what it would have found.

At first Mr Baker wanted sponsors to put up £8 million towards capital costs, but it rapidly became clear that they were not going to put up anything like that amount of money, and the figure was quietly forgotten. Mr Baker made it known that he would accept £2 million and be grateful. The Government would happily stump up the rest, on average about £10 million. But even though the Government was now paying most of the capital costs and all the running costs, the sponsor would still own the CTC.

As it happens, £2 million was the figure New Labour decided on for city academies 14 years later, though of course £2 million was worth far less by then, and was a far smaller proportion of the total cost. And, as Mr Baker had done, New Labour was to find that it was more than most sponsors wanted to pay. But we run ahead of ourselves.

In order to attract sponsors, Mr Baker said that business people were welcome to name their colleges after themselves or their companies, and that they could dictate the curriculum. It was to be the ultimate sponsorship opportunity: to be known as a company which cared about education, to have your name and logo engraved on the hearts of millions of schoolchildren, and even to ensure that they were taught the skills your company required.

Yet it was not enough. IBM, ICI, the banks, Marks & Spencer and other household-name companies all said no. Mrs Thatcher herself had to be called in to try to twist the arms of top business people, personally telephoning the chairman of BP. BP's then educational adviser Jeremy Nicholls told me why, even then, the company resisted the Prime Minister's blandishments:

Companies with a strong tradition of local community support and partnership have tended not to support CTCs. The problem is that companies want to make friends in the communities where they operate. They do not support high-profile initiatives which are seen by many people in the community as divisive. There was a feeling that CTCs were going to focus a lot of resources on a few children. We want UK plc to invest in the future of all its children.

We were also unhappy about the confusion of an education agenda with a political agenda. The country needs to find means of educating more people to a higher level. The taxpayer at large is the proper person to do that, rather than the BP shareholder.

Try re-reading that, replacing 'CTCs' with 'city academies'. It sounds remarkably contemporary. And Mr Nicholls' judgements are as valid today as they were then.

So CTC sponsors tended to be smaller companies, headed by the sort of businessman whose admirers call entrepreneurial, and whose enemies call him nothing at all unless their lawyers are present. Mr Michael Ashcroft was chairman of Bermuda-registered security services company ADT and a guarantor of the Conservative Party's overdraft, and paid just £1 million to sponsor the ADT city technology college in Wandsworth, which his company owns and controls to this day, though the taxpayer pays the bills. In January 1990 he made it clear how his business interests and Wandworth Council's politics could be made to benefit, in a private letter to council leader Sir Paul Beresford:

> From a political point of view the higher the profile that can be given to the creation of the CTC concept here in Wandsworth the better, and no doubt this will be of much help to your local Conservative candidates for the May 1990 elections.
>
> I have therefore suggested to the Prime Minister and Kenneth Baker that it would be helpful if a small ceremony could be held on or around 2 April 1990 so that the college can be formally handed over . . . to the new CTC Trust. The Prime Minister's presence would of course guarantee publicity.

You might wonder whether a tobacco company ought to be sponsoring a school, but British American Tobacco's money was gratefully accepted in Middlesbrough – a town which has again found itself the centre of controversy with its city academies, as we will see.

In Lewisham, south London, the sponsor, the Haberdashers Company, did not actually part with a single penny. Since it was already running a state school on the site, it 'gave' the site to the new CTC. The CTC Trust valued the site in the region of £2 million. This arrangement, as we shall find, took an even more bizarre turn with the advent of city academies.

Sometimes even creative accounting was not enough. Brighton property speculator Ivor Revere's aborted CTC in Sussex triggered a National Audit Office investigation after it was discovered that he had paid £2.3 million for the site and charged the taxpayer £2.5 million for it. After Mr Revere's withdrawal the Government was left with a disused Sussex school the value of which was declining. It was still unsold four years later, in 1993, and was costing £1,000 a week for Group 4 Security to look after it.

Labour quickly realized that the idea was a dud. Labour's then education spokesman Jack Straw told the House of Commons: 'No programme has been such a comprehensive and expensive failure . . . [It] is wasteful and wrong, so why does he [the Education Secretary] not scrap it altogether and immediately save £120 million, which could be spent on a crash programme of repairs and improvements, as we have demanded?'[1] He was horrified that the Government was spending many times as much money on each CTC pupil as on state school pupils.

He called Kenneth Baker 'the architect of the lethal combination of city technology colleges, opting out, the local management of schools, an inflexible national curriculum, and the constant denigration of the teaching profession which has brought the service so low'. Every one of these has continued under the Government of which Mr Straw has been a member since 1997. I'm not aware that Mr Straw has made any protest at all.

He added: 'Is not the truth of the city technology programme that financial controls have been so inadequate that Ministers and donors have been able to play fast and loose with public funds?'

By July 1990 Mr Straw was able to point out that only a fraction of the private sector money which had been promised had actually been delivered. Exactly the same has happened with academies, though you will search in vain for any mention of the fact from Mr Straw.

Perhaps his deadliest attack was a 1990 press release in which he said that sponsors were 'second-order companies whose directors were interested in political leverage or honours'. In the case of city academies, we have had to discover this for ourselves, without Mr Straw's assistance.

In 1989, Margaret Hodge, the Labour chair of the Association of London Authorities, said that the next Labour Government should return all the CTCs to local authority control. Ms Hodge has been a New Labour luminary throughout the life of the New Labour Government, and has even served a stint in the DfES.

'Pupils', said Mr Baker, 'will span the full range of ability.' But almost in the same breath he added: 'They will be selected on the basis of their aptitude, their readiness to take advantage of the type of education offered in CTCs, and their parents' commitment to full-time education up to the age of 18 and to the CTC curriculum and ethos.'

In practice, at first, this allowed CTCs to interview children with both parents, and, so long as they selected from across all ability bands, they could choose the children they thought would be easy to teach, and whose parents were likely to co-operate and not make waves.

A businessman, Cyril Taylor, was appointed to head the CTC Trust. Today, now Sir Cyril (knighted for services to education), he heads the Trust which promotes city academies.

I was shown around the first CTC, Kingshurst, near Birmingham. The spacious classrooms, full of the latest technology, would have turned a teacher in most state schools green with envy. The brochure was glossy and expensive. Nearby stood crumbling, decaying, cash-starved schools for the pupils who could not get into Kingshurst. Its sponsor, the automotive company GKN, had a manager in the school to advise the head and the teachers on teaching and curriculum matters, though he had no experience of education.

Its first head teacher, Valerie Bragg, later decamped to run a private education company, Three Es. Under her successor, Ann Jones, Kingshurst is going to become a city academy, though this will not require any changes, just the ability to absorb some more public money which state schools need far more urgently. Kingshurst concentrates on vocational subjects, especially engineering, and Ms Jones insists that the fact that the sponsors are engineering companies is entirely coincidental.

That was to be a mark of CTCs, as it is of city academies: that they were to teach vocational subjects. Cyril Taylor spelled it out with a characteristic directness and honesty which is absent from New Labour statements about academies. 'Employers are telling me that the schools do not teach the skills that they require. In the CTCs that they fund, they will ensure that the correct skills are taught.' Mr Baker admitted that such things as arts subjects might suffer in the CTCs. These were to be hothouses for the worker bees of industry.

The last CTC to be authorized, in April 1991, was Kingswood in Bristol. After the by now familiar scramble for a bit of private sector cash to make the thing look respectable, the

chairman of Cable and Wireless and former Tory Party
chairman Lord Young stumped up the required £2 million. The
Government gratefully handed over the other £8 million. Avon
County Council's deputy director of education, Edward
Watson, bitterly contrasted that £8 million for capital spending
on the 900 children at Kingswood with the £4.5 million which
he had for capital spending on the county's other 150,000
children. With the extra money, he said, all secondary schools in
Kingswood could be fully repaired, all improvements they asked
for could be done, all could have a new science laboratory, and
there would be enough left over to give all primary schools an
extra nursery class for a year.

Mr Watson was unlucky. If he had been able to hold out for
just a few months more, he would never have had a CTC on his
patch. For by then, while a new Education Secretary, Kenneth
Clarke, was blustering about the success of CTCs, he was
actually in headlong retreat. Kingswood was the fifteenth and
last CTC. The very next one to be proposed, in Barnet, north
London, was quietly vetoed by Mr Clarke, and no more were
considered. This is the nearest politicians ever get to saying
'Sorry, that policy was a dud.'

But nine years later, in March 2000, David Blunkett, the
New Labour Education Secretary, announced the revival of the
policy, and called it city academies.

By then, New Labour had been in power for three years, and
was not looking as though it was minded to change much of
Conservative education policy. It had even had a go at getting
private sector sponsorship, with Mr Blunkett's ill-fated Education Action Zones (EAZs), launched in 1998. If the history of
CTCs had not taught New Labour that the private sector was
not keen on putting loads of money into state education, the
searing experience of EAZs should have done so.

Mr Blunkett obtained glitzy presentations for his EAZs from 47 local consortia at a total cost to the taxpayer of just under £1 million. Each one had to show him that they could raise money from private enterprise to fund an EAZ, designed to raise standards of the schools within it. If they could convince him of this, he would bung them £750,000 a year for three years.

So, of course, they set out to convince him. He made it as easy as he could. He said that business contributions could be 'in kind' – perhaps the services of a superannuated executive to sit on committees.

And this is the sort of thing he got.

North-east Derbyshire's consortium said that the local NatWest bank is 'unfortunately not in a position to be able to offer any financial support' but will be glad to continue its help in kind. So, for example, more head teachers would be offered the opportunity afforded to John Young, who 'has recently benefited from a teacher placement with Paul Adcock, NatWest's area business manager'.

The Post Office offered 'talks on professional skills for teachers/school staff/governors' and 'telephone/customer answering techniques (interpersonal skills) for students'. It has future call centre staff to think about.

At Ellesmere Port, Associated Octel offered 'to make the facilities of the Learning Centre open to local schools, providing hi-tech learning opportunities'. This was calculated as a £70,000 donation. The local branch of Barclays Bank offered to send someone to sit on the 'forum' that controls the zone and asked for volunteers from its staff to sit on school governing bodies. It also offered 'mentoring/contribution to training of staff especially regarding banking and financial matters' and work placements. The bid valued the Barclays contribution at £30,000.

A Bradford company allowed two managers to give occasional advice, and Bradford's grateful Action Zone called that £5,000 a year. The Blue Planet Aquarium in Ellesmere Port offered half-price entrance for Zone pupils: there, that's another £12,500 donation.

In Newham, east London, the construction giants Mowlem and Laing agreed to take Action Zone pupils to their offices and tell them about how splendid it was to work in construction (an industry with an acute recruitment crisis). This went down as a £40,000 donation.

At last, at the end of 2001, it fell to the luckless junior minister Stephen Timms to announce that the Government was pulling the plug on EAZs. Even then, he claimed that it had brought into education £37 million from the private sector, without mentioning that nearly all of that was the sort of pretend money described above. It was a pretty poor return for a public investment of £57 million. If that money had gone straight into education, it would have done some good.

So Mr Blunkett did not have to look back at the sad history of Mr Baker's CTCs to know that business was not keen on coughing up money to help state education. He had discovered this for himself. Nonetheless, he went ahead with city academies, provided for in the Learning and Skills Act which received royal assent on 27 July 2000.

They grew out of the 'fresh start' project – the idea that failing schools could be closed and replaced by a new school. Failing schools were defined as those which for three consecutive years failed to achieve five A* to C grades at GCSE for at least 15 per cent of pupils. Academies were, Blunkett said, 'a radical approach to promote greater diversity and break the cycle of failing schools in inner cities'. They would either replace an existing school or schools, or meet a demand for new places. The aim was 'to challenge the culture of educational underattainment'. Each academy had to have a sponsor. Sponsors could be 'businesses, individuals, churches and other faith groups, or voluntary bodies'.

They were CTCs in all but name. The only difference is that sponsors of academies are even freer to decide what to do. They are no longer restricted to urban areas, nor to secondary schools. Academies can be all-age schools, and can specialize in any subject or combination of subjects.

And, of course, they had a new name. There's a sort of creeping gentrification about the names we give to our schools. Mr Baker in 1986 obviously thought that the word 'school' sounded a bit proletarian, and called his new schools 'colleges', enabling them to sound like Eton College or Winchester College. But, of course, the very act of doing so devalued the snob value of the world 'college' and Mr Blunkett had to find a new one. Now that he has devalued 'academy' where do we go next? I have a small side bet on 'conservatoire'.

However – as Mr Blunkett might have said, and probably did – it's easy to sneer. Academies are tackling deep-seated problems. If it works, it works. And if it works, why should we care that the idea seems silly, that we cannot find a decent reason for bringing in sponsors, that it is a warmed-up Conservative policy, or even that ministers cannot explain it without falling back on dead management jargon? Success is its own justification. If it works, that would be justification enough.

So has it worked?

Note
1. Jack Straw, 20 May 1988.

2

Blunkett Throws Money at Academies

If ministers' willingness to get behind a project were enough to make it work, city academies would be a roaring success. Just a week after Blunkett announced the project, on 23 March 2000, he was able to tell the world that he had £60 million of Government money to plough into it. By the end of July the legislation had royal assent. On 15 September he announced his first three academies, on 12 October two more, and yet another on 18 December.

The first three academies opened in September 2002. Nine more opened a year later, and a further five in September 2004, two months after the Government announced its target of 200 academies by 2010.

He was setting a breakneck pace, so fast that most people did not see what was going on. Looking back, we can see how it was done, and whether there was anything which might, even at that late stage, have alerted ministers to the lurking disaster.

Academies were to get their running costs direct from the Government, bypassing the local authority, so that they could be fully independent. This, said Blunkett, would 'allow them the flexibility to be innovative and creative in their curriculum, staffing and governance'.

Now, if such independence is a good thing, every school should have it, unless the school can be shown to be incompetently run. Why was it confined to academies?

The same applied in other areas. Academies were to be exempt from the National Curriculum. There were no set pay scales; sponsors could pay staff what they liked and set what employment conditions they liked, since staff were not employed within the framework of the Schoolteachers Pay and Conditions Act 1991. Whatever the sponsor decided, the public purse would pick up the bill. Sponsors were to get the entire school budget direct from the Government.

This may be one of the reasons why costs rocketed. At first academies were said to be going to cost £10 million each, which made the sponsor's £2 million sound like a respectable contribution. The average for each of the first 12 was £23 million, and later ones have cost a lot more than that (though costs are now being belatedly reined in). The Bexley Business Academy, the most expensive of the lot, had a capital budget of £35.9 million, and has easily overspent on it. The sponsor's contribution has remained capped at £2 million. All future costs will come from the public purse. In August 2004 the *Times Educational Supplement* revealed that half the 12 academies that were open by summer 2004 had yet to receive the full £2 million from sponsors.

And that's ignoring all the money spent to try to prove, in each area, that the academy was the only way forward. Each time, there is development money of hundreds of thousands of pounds so that the sponsor can write a proposal. And even before that, there is an army of DfES-funded consultants, for whom the Government advertised right at the start at a rate of £300 a day, to work on such things as 'curriculum innovation for high performance' and 'the management of change' and other fashionable bits of feelgood management jargon.

Academies were even, at first, exempt from the requirement for maintained school teachers to register with the General

Teaching Council. This council was set up in the same year as academies to deal with cases of professional misconduct and incompetence, and to reassure parents that their children were being taught by competent and trustworthy people. Blunkett said: 'The Council will have a significant role in raising the morale of teachers, raising standards in our classrooms and modernizing the profession.' But, announcing that academies were to be free of it, Lord Filkin, Blunkett's spokesman in the House of Lords, said academies needed to be free of 'the regulatory constraints, burdens and bureaucracy of the maintained sector (of education)'.

Either registration with the GTC raises teaching standards, in which case every school's teachers should have to register; or it is a 'constraint, burden and bureaucracy' in which case it should be abolished. There is no case for having it, and letting academies alone ignore it.

This last decision was eventually reversed, not because the Government saw the contradiction, but because the GTC pointed out forcibly to ministers that they were giving it a pretty poor start in life. They could not tell it to go out and show the world that it was a force for good; and then exclude the Government's flagship schools. It's surprising, and an indication of the haste with which things were being done, that ministers had not thought of this for themselves.

The Government allowed academies to select 10 per cent of their intake by 'aptitude', breaking its pledge that there was to be no more selection in secondary education. In 2005, almost half of the 27 academies were doing so.

The pace accelerated. Nine more were opened in 2003, five in 2004 and ten in 2005. As I write this (October 2006) there are 46, and the Government is aiming for 200.

The Government was pumping £20 million to £30 million

into each new academy. Later it started spending as much as £38 million[1] – and in one case, Bexley, more than £50 million. To most state schools, that is undreamed-of riches, enough to furnish them with everything they ever wanted. There was no increase in sponsors' £2 million, and many sponsors, as we shall see, have put in less than half that sum. Even if they did put in the full £2 million, the real cost to them, when tax incentives are taken into account, is more like £1.2 million. Sponsors were also able, unchecked, to channel public money into their own companies.

A pupil place at an academy costs £21,000, almost twice as much as the cost of a pupil place at another state school, which is just under £14,000.[2]

What all this adds up to is that the Government seems not simply to have wanted academies to be good: it wanted other schools to be worse than academies. It seems to have wanted a cadre of schools to which everyone locally aspired to go, and other schools which taught their rejects – schools with a fraction as much money, and without the freedoms which the Government considered necessary if a school was to excel.

The Government was warned that this huge concentration of resources in a few schools was unlikely even to achieve the limited objective of making a very few schools very good. The warning came, not from that old enemy the teaching unions, but from its own private sector consultants. A Government-commissioned report from PricewaterhouseCoopers said academies could lead to a two-tier system based on social class, and they were not producing innovative teaching. When given greater autonomy, said the report, some schools return to traditional values and implement a curriculum with a strong emphasis on 'back to basics'. Academies showed signs of doing this.

The report was given to ministers in November 2003, and instantly suppressed. The Government did not release its contents until forced to do so two years later under the Freedom of Information Act by the *Times Educational Supplement*. But its reasoning was the same as that of the Government's favourite tycoon, Sir Peter Lampl, whose Sutton Trust has put money and enthusiasm into state education, and researches how best to do it. Lampl thought that the idea was a dud from the start, and refused to have anything to do with it. He says:

> I don't think you should be putting large amounts of money into new buildings. Sometimes a new building with the right sponsor may be the right answer, but often the buildings are quite all right, you just need to spend some money to fix them up. We have funded over 30 specialist schools where for a total capital investment of £150,000 (£50,000 from the sponsors and £100,000 from the Government) and extra funding of approximately £100,000 per year from the Government, some spectacular results have been achieved. For instance, at the Phoenix School in Hammersmith, GCSEs have gone from 28 per cent in 2003 to 77 per cent today.

The House of Commons Select Committee issued a report saying that there was no reason to suppose academies were going to raise the standard of education. Many were not doing so, the role of sponsors was a worry, and the Government should stop after 30 or 50 and assess them.

Remember BP's educational adviser on city technology colleges? 'We do not support high-profile initiatives which are seen by many people in the community as divisive. There was a feeling that these schools were going to focus a lot of resources on a few children.' New Labour in 2000 was making exactly the same mistake as the Conservatives had made in 1986. Not surprisingly, BP has not sponsored any city academies. Neither have any other household-name companies.

The control of the sponsor is almost absolute. The sponsor appoints a majority of the governing body. Academies are only required to have one parent governor and only one staff governor. There is no requirement to have a single teacher on it – teachers may be represented by another staff member.

The only other possible check on the power of the sponsor – the only remaining democratric control – is the local council, and this has been carefully and thoroughly stripped out. The Government's stated intention is to change the role of local councils from providers to 'commissioners' of education – commissioning other organizations to build and run schools. Once a local council has 'commissioned' an academy, it can do nothing about the way it works.

So the only power your elected councillors have is the power to decide not to go down the academy route. And they have in effect been stripped of that power, too. When ministers tell us there must be something in academies because so many local councils choose to have them, they are telling us a terrible fib. It is like saying that people must have liked the poll tax because so many of them paid it.

Effectively, local authorities were being told: give up your power to any business mogul who wants an academy on your patch, or we will starve your area of education funding, and your residents can watch their children's schools rot. Their choice is this. They can set up academies, and get money from central Government to rebuild and refurbish schools. Or they can reject the Government's academies, in which case they get no money for school building and refurbishment.

It's a kind of protection racket, and this is how it works.

Money for school building is now allocated under an initiative called Building Schools for the Future (BSF). It is no longer simply a matter of finding the money and then building or refurbishing a school. A local authority now normally has to obtain funds through a local BSF project, run by a Local Education Partnership (LEP). An LEP is a joint-venture company, controlled by contractors who are awarded a ten-year contract, and in which the contractor (a private company) has 80 per cent control. This means, of course, that a private company could be both bidding for work from a local council, and acting as an adviser to the council on the work at the same time.

To get their hands on any money for school building, the council must show the Government its so-called Strategy for Change. And it has only to look on the DfES website to find out what is expected of this strategy. Here is what it will find:

The following questions are provided in order to help local authorities ensure they have properly considered Academies within their Strategy for Change:

a. To what extent has the local authority objectively and proactively considered academies as an alternative option where it proposes to rebuild poorly performing state schools?

b. Where a local authority is proposing to rebuild or substantially refurbish a poorly performing maintained school . . . and is not proposing an academy, has the authority explained why an academy is not being proposed . . . ?

c. If an authority has not considered an academy when proposing a new school in an area of deprivation what has been the rationale?

d. Has there been an early clarification of the options for academies with the DfES?

e. How does the local authority policy ensure that academies, including their specialisms, are positive contributors to the local networks of educational provision?

The message is clear enough: it's most unlikely that any excuse for failing to go down the academies route will be good enough. But just in case there's any misunderstanding, the document adds: 'Academies – and new or reformed schools including academy features – should form a key part pf BSF plans.' A couple of sentences later: 'The Government will expect local authorities to provide a proper and objective evaluation of academy options.' And then: 'The Government will not stand by and allow local authorities to sustain failure by refusing to engage with academies.' This is one of those verbal tricks which distinguish New Labour propaganda. No academies = 'sustaining failure'.

If it's worth saying once, it's worth repeating until councils get the message. So a sentence further on we read: 'The DfES would expect to see proposals for the establishment of an academy where a local authority is proposing to rebuild or substantially refurbish a poorly performing maintained school.' The next paragraph says: 'Local authorities should therefore consider the scope for establishing academies . . . Plans containing bold innovation in the use of academies . . . will be more likely to raise standards, and therefore more likely to progress quickly through . . . to the final approval of funding.' And the next one says: 'Local authorities are encouraged to engage directly with academy sponsors . . .' It would be a very dim-witted councillor who failed to get the message.

Some local authorities have been told, explicitly, that their BSF funding depended on including academies in their plans. Councils elected specifically on a platform of no academies in

Newcastle upon Tyne, Birmingham, and Camden and Islington in north London, have effectively been told that what their voters say does not matter in the slightest, and have been forced to go for academies. The maxim seems to be: if the voters don't like the policy, change the voters. Liverpool NUT Secretary Ruth Knox protested in 2002: 'The people here are being told you won't get anything done unless you allow your two schools to be demolished. They are saying: get this or get nothing. In effect they are being blackmailed.'

Having once agreed to an academy in their patch, the council hands all control over what it does to the sponsor. A council's strategic plan for education in its area means very little to many academy sponsors. They have all followed the Government's helpful suggestion that they ensure the sponsor has an inbuilt majority on the governing body, and they do what they like. No council with an academy on its patch can plan for education as a whole. We will see later on the muddle this creates.

By September 2005 there were 27 academies, almost half of them selecting 10 per cent of their pupils by 'aptitude'. Sponsors, though they were to dictate the buildings and control the teaching, were not required to have any educational expertise and experience. The specialism reflects their interests. Parents have no say at all. If a football club or a sports equipment mogul is in charge, the specialism is generally sport. Nearly half the academies offer business and enterprise as their specialism. Sport and technology are also popular, but shortage subjects like modern foreign languages, maths and science are less well served.

Even with these extraordinary powers, sponsors have been hard to find, as we shall see in the next chapter.

Notes

1. NUT Briefing, *Academies: Looking Beyond the Spin*, 2006.
2. Parliamentary Select Committee on Education and Skills, March 2005.

3

Sponsors in Ermine

One trouble with city technology colleges, said Labour's education spokesman Jack Straw in 1990, was that sponsors were 'second order companies whose directors were interested in political leverage or honours'.

When Labour reinvented CTCs and called them city academies, exactly the same thing happened, only on a far bigger scale and in a much more organized way. The scheme became entwined with the growingly controversial area of political party funding. The chief fundraiser for city academies is Lord Levy, who is president of the Specialist Schools and Academies Trust (SSAT) – and also chief fundraiser for New Labour. Of course, he may have kept these two jobs in separate compartments – this morning I am fundraising for the Labour Party, this afternoon I shall be fundraising for the city academy programme – but that looks like a pretty hard trick to bring off. No doubt by coincidence, the SSAT took splendid offices with wonderful views over the Thames in Millbank Tower – the same building in which New Labour had its offices until recently. Lord Levy's journey between the two organizations was not therefore an onerous one.

Lord Levy is also Tony Blair's unofficial envoy to the Middle East. He met Blair at a dinner party in 1994 held by a senior Israeli diplomat, and became his tennis partner. Levy was in charge of donations to the 'private trust' which funded Tony Blair's office before the 1997 election (which reached £7 million), and is now the chief fundraiser for the 'high value' donors' account at the Labour Party. He is reported to have raised £12 million for the 'high value' fund before the 1997 election. Straight after the election he was given a peerage.

He set up Magnet Records in 1972 with help from Maurice Oberstein, head of CBS Records, and made millions from artists like Alvin Stardust, Chris Rea and Bad Manners. He sold Magnet to Warner Brothers in 1988 for £10 million and later set up another record company called M&G (named after himself and his wife Gilda). He sold M&G in 1997.

All the big household-name companies have turned down the Government's blandishments and refused to support academies – even those companies which do support education. That leaves a ragbag of second-hand car salesmen, evangelical Christians, advertising agencies, churches, property speculators and a few others, some of whom want to put up as little money as possible, and get as much control as possible for it. The former UK head of Enron, listed by the Specialist Schools Trust as a specialist school donor, said that sponsorship and donations were the best way of getting access to ministers.[1] Some want a place where young people can be taught their potty religious notions, others a training ground for their future staff, others still a PR bonus – and some, it has to be said, are honestly sure they are doing good.

Their interests are reflected in the very large proportion of academies which have business and enterprise as their specialism. Seven of the 46 have it as the sole specialism, and another 19 have it as one of two or three specialisms, making 26 in all with a business and enterprise specialism – well over half. The CBI and the World Bank have both identified education as a future, untapped area for commercial exploitation, and several sponsors – including the biggest, the United Learning Trust – also run fee-charging private schools.

£2 million, a fraction of the likely capital cost of an academy, turned out to be far too much, even though the state was going to pick up the tab for the running costs in perpetuity. Quite soon, the money expected from sponsors had quietly become 'up to £2 million'. From being the minimum, £2 million overnight became the maximum.

And then, ever so quietly, three dread words were added: 'in cash *or in kind*'. We've heard this before. Help 'in kind' means almost anything. The services of an elderly executive, too senior to fire and too tired to be of any use, who can sit on committees, and the value of whose time, generously estimated, can be marked down as a generous contribution to our beleaguered education system.

There are sponsors who do put in the full amount. But even if they do so, £2 million is still a drop in the ocean – especially when you remember that a corporation can claim tax relief for the money, reducing their real contribution to an estimated £1.2 million.

So what do sponsors contribute, if not money? The Specialist Schools Trust (as it then was, before it took over the Academies Trust and became the SSAT) explained. A sponsor, it said, will 'animate the academy's vision, ethos and management structures'. Yes, it's in that much trouble. You don't fall back on entirely meaningless management jargon until things are really bad.

Churches have also been targeted. Tony Blair's ubiquitous education adviser Andrew Adonis, the powerhouse behind the policy and now Lord Adonis and an education minister, went to a meeting of the General Synod and told them that the Church of England should become a major partner in 57 academies. The *Times Educational Supplement* reported in February 2004 that Adonis thought it would be one way in which the church could reach its target of 100 new faith schools.

Some pretty desperate stratagems have been tried. In October 2002, schools standards minister David Miliband made an appeal to private fee-charging schools. 'The Eton Academy, the Winchester Academy – it has a certain ring to it', he said cheerfully. The Government seems to think that these schools, because of their years of experience of educating a wealthy élite, can teach the state sector how to educate the poorest inner-city children.

There were the germs of a grubby little deal in the making here. Fee-charging schools are, absurdly, classed as charities, and at the time there were still mutterings about charitable status being taken away from them. But they took the hint that if they got involved in 'community projects' they would be all right. Graham Able, then chairman of the top public schools' club, the Headmasters and Headmistresses Conference, said public schools were ready to help start academies. Oundle (fees for boarders £21,518, for day pupils £13,185 a year) showed interest in setting up an academy specializing in technology and science.

But the Government's known reluctance to do anything about their charitable status in any case left ministers in a weak bargaining position. The very splendid north London girls' school, North London Collegiate (fees £10,518 a year), announced in 2003 that it would sponsor an academy. Nothing came of this, but headmistress Bernice McCabe says today that she is still willing to respond to Government requests. Mr Able's own school, Dulwich College in south London (fees £12,060 a year) showed an interest in sponsoring an academy in 2004, and is providing 'support in kind' to the Isle of Sheppey's new academy.

Millfield School, an independent school in Street, has formed a partnership with Bristol City Academy, but it does not involve handing over money. Millfield gets good links with Bristol City Football Club and in return Millfield helps the academy to get its students into university. The partnership also covers theatre studies co-operation and gifted and talented student exchanges.

The *TES* reported on 13 August 2004: 'The private sponsors running these projects have in some cases spent very little of their own money and a great deal of the public's to build schools at costs far exceeding what any local education authority – working under strict government guidelines – is allowed to spend.'

By April 2005, desperation to find private sponsors had reached fever pitch, so much so that the Government adopted the cheap huckster's trick of a cut-rate offer if you buy more than three. Sponsors have been told that if they fund three academies, the 'price' for each one thereafter will be only £1.5 million rather than the standard £2 million.

In return for that upfront cash towards the capital costs of the new school, sponsors are given more or less absolute control of the curriculum, ethos and staffing. The Government will provide the remainder of the money for the new school, typically about £23 million.

But perhaps the record deal was the one the Haberdashers Company got. Back in the dying days of city technology colleges, the Conservative Government invented a system of smoke and mirrors which the academies programme has been swift to build on. In Lewisham, south London, the sponsor, the Haberdashers Company, a city livery company whose charter goes back to the sixteenth century, did not actually part with a single penny. Since it was already running a state school on the site, it 'gave' the site to the new CTC. The CTC Trust valued a new 99-year lease on the land and buildings at more than

£2 million, and, magically, another generous and public-spirited sponsor had come forward.

The local education authority had put a lot of money into those buildings over the years, but they got not a penny to spend on Lewisham's other schools. While the CTC was given £5.5 million from the Government for further improvements, Lewisham's other 16 schools had £1.2 million to share between them.

Today, that city technology college is to become a city academy, owned and controlled by the Haberdashers, benefiting from another large dollop of taxpayers' cash, and taking over another local school. The Haberdashers Company is still not keen on putting up money. Anything Kenneth Clarke can do, Charles Clarke can also do, and just before he left the Department for Education, the new academy went up on the department website. 'The main sponsor', it said, 'is the Haberdashers' Livery Company.' So how much, I wondered, was the sponsor putting in this time, in return for control of two schools instead of one? The council told me it does not know; the school said no one there can discuss it; the Haberdashers Company said only the school can discuss it. The relevant paragraph in the funding agreement is secret, and the Government successfully blocked a request to see it under the Freedom of Information Act. Local rumour puts the figure somewhere in the region of peanuts. Lawyer Richard Stein managed to get the figure. Haberdashers is putting in just £295,500 out of a total cost of just over £38 million.

Another former CTC had been started in Bradford with sponsorship from Dixons, the electrical retailers, and called Dixons College. Dixons does not want to sponsor the new academy proposed there. But a city technology college is an independent school – so what's to stop it sponsoring itself?

Up on the DfES website went the agreement: the new academy 'will be sponsored by Dixons College, which will be providing sponsorship of £395,000'.

Yet another former CTC, the Djanogly CTC in Nottingham, worked much the same trick. The sponsor, Sir Harry Djanogly, put in not a penny, and the Government put in £21.2 million when it became an academy in September 2003. The excuse was that, in 1989, he found £2 million for the CTC which the new academy replaces.

At one point things got so desperate that the DfES website was inventing sponsors. It said the Macmillan Trust – the charitable arm of the famous publishing house – was going to sponsor an academy in Middlesbrough, but the Macmillan Trust was only then being approached, and it turned the idea down.

In Barnet, north London, Peter Shalson, director of a venture capital company, is only required to put in £1.5 million. The excuse is that some of the playing fields of the school his academy will replace are being sold for development, which will bring in the other half-million.

In April 2006 the luckless Des Smith, a council member of the Specialist Schools and Academies Trust (SSAT), was caught promising that honours could be lined up for supporters of the academy programme. The *Sunday Times* reported that Mr Smith told a journalist posing as a potential donor's PR assistant: 'The prime minister's office would recommend someone like [the donor] for an OBE, a CBE or a knighthood.' Asked if this would be just for getting involved in the academies, he responded: 'Yes . . . they call them services to education. I would say to Cyril's office that we've got to start writing to the prime minister's office.' For a donation of £10 million, 'You could go to the House of Lords.'

'Cyril' here is Sir Cyril Taylor, whom we first met running the CTC programme after 1986, and who now runs the SSAT. He rushed to tell the world that Mr Smith was terribly low-level, he didn't know anything, and the silly fellow got carried away. He did not know if Mr Smith had ever met Lord Levy, though he thought he probably had.

He did not mention that Mr Smith was one of his carefully chosen guests at a lunch to meet the *Sunday Times* reporter; Sir Cyril, too, thought she was the PRO to a multi-millionaire. Other guests included Sir Michael Barber, former head of delivery at 10 Downing Street, two multi-millionaire business-men, two representatives of an American multinational, and Rona Kiley, wife of London's transport commissioner Bob Kiley and the academy sponsorship consultant.

Mr Smith was not quite the ignorant nonentity Sir Cyril likes to make out. Sir Cyril himself had been more guarded than Mr Smith, but he had said to the reporter: 'There's no question that sponsors of academies have access, they get invited to No. 10, meet the Secretary of State and people like that. Some people say "I'm going to buy a knighthood doing this" but I think they should not think that at all because, first of all, that's a form of corruption. But the fact is a lot of sponsors do get recognition.'[2] The SSAT was paying Mr Smith £500 a day on top of his £80,000 a year head teacher's salary, and he now bitterly regrets taking it.

The SSAT official statement said:

Mr Smith's involvement with the SSAT was limited solely to educational matters. He was engaged as a consultant by SSAT to provide school improvement advice in relation to academies on two specific projects (which necessitated two days' work), and he also acted as a consultant to the

Department for Education and Skills, to provide educational input on two other projects in Bristol and in London.

The Metropolitan Police, the statement confirmed, had asked
SSAT to assist them in their enquiries.

Even the Defence Secretary joined in the rush to tell the
world what an inconsequential fellow Mr Smith was. John Reid
said on television: 'I don't know who Mr Des Smith is . . . He
doesn't speak with any authority for the Government at all. As
far as I'm aware, he doesn't speak for the Labour Party either.'
Schools Minister David Miliband, who had singled him out
and brought him to the platform during a major conference
designed to display New Labour's successes, disowned him.
As he and Mr Reid washed their hands of him, the insignificant
Mr Smith was dragged from his bed in a dawn raid by police
and thrown in a cell.

It was a miserable end to a distinguished teaching career. A
teacher all his life, Mr Smith had successfully turned round a
troubled East End school, and then become one of the Government's 'superheads', charged with going to schools and helping
them out of trouble. Towards the end of his teaching career he
had been taken up by Sir Cyril as a suitable head teacher to
introduce to potential sponsors, and had worked with the
company Capita. These contacts took him to the unfamiliar
world of London's best restaurants and the company of top
politicians and businessmen, and – fatally – introduced him to
the attractive young woman from the *Sunday Times* posing as a
PR for a multi-millionaire.

The last year of his career, 2006, when he reached the age of
60, should have been a time to retire heaped with well-earned
praise. But his retirement has not been like that. He retired

quietly, under a cloud, with none of the ceremonies he might have expected. At the time of writing, his case was supposed to come to court on 12 October 2006, but it has been deferred and his bail has been extended.

As so often, it's the foot-soldiers who suffer while the generals disown them; and the foot-soldiers are ill-equipped to protect themselves. Mr Smith, having fallen for the sting of an attractive young woman journalist from the *Sunday Times*, told his troubles to a man who had befriended him, and who worked for the *Mail on Sunday*. The Government which had used him and disowned him did not bother to try to protect him from his lack of media experience. In the *Mail on Sunday*, Mr Smith's anguish was bared to the world. I understand he was not paid a penny for his story.

The paper published it on 3 December 2006. Mr Smith told how 'police presented him with a "gong list" of 43 public figures who had received honours under New Labour; how the Labour establishment disowned him despite his lifetime of public service; how he was caught drink-driving as he headed for a nervous breakdown and considered committing suicide.' For good measure he added that 'Millions of pounds have been squandered in the city academies programme.'

He said:

As a citizen I am equal to Tony Blair. I need him to be treated the same way. If you are sitting in Chequers surrounded by your advisers, it might be quite a comfortable interview. I demand that Blair is arrested at 10 Downing Street at 7.20am, that he is taken to a police station – hopefully Stoke Newington, which is a very unpleasant Bastille-type place – and treated in the same way that I have been treated.

He spent most of the day in the cell. 'When I finally left the police station in mid-afternoon' he told the *Mail on Sunday*,

> the officers said they would drop me off. But my wife rang and said 'Don't come home. There are television cameras here and dozens of journalists.' . . . The difference between David Kelly [the weapons inspector who committed suicide over the Iraq weapons of mass destruction affair] and myself is that he did it. I couldn't do it. There is a big difference between wanting to die and actually killing yourself.

What is his view about academies now? 'Money has been wasted in the most appalling way. Many of them are the same schools with the same problems, just with new buildings. The people [Blair] has applauded are the businessmen and the guys in the City who earn all the money. The nurses and the teachers have been abandoned.'

But by then, six academy sponsors had been honoured under Labour, and three more had been offered peerages, only to see the offer withdrawn when newspapers started to talk about buying honours. They were deemed unsuitable to be peers. 'It seems strange therefore', comments the NUT's booklet *Academies: Looking Beyond the Spin*, 'that they have been deemed to be suitable to sponsor academies and consequently have considerable influence over pupils' education in these academies.' Most people believe that Mr Smith was simply reflecting the prevailing culture of the SSAT.

Even with this sort of inducement, sponsors proved very hard to find. A few expressed an interest, only to withdraw as they saw the depth of local hostility. And those who stayed were remarkably reluctant to part with cash. In May 2006 the *Guardian* reported that most of them had not paid the £2 million. Four academies which had been open for nearly a year had not received a penny from their sponsor. With 27 academies up and running, sponsors had paid up only £26 million.

It's partly for this reason that, just as this book was going to press, the Government suddenly announced a revolution in the way the academy programme is run. I say 'announced'; actually it did the exact opposite: it let the information out in paragraph 10 of a press release headed *Parent power and new independent report give fresh backing to academies.* The first nine paragraphs were a non-story about how academies must be wonderful because parents couldn't get their children into some of them. The tenth paragraph began 'Also announced today is a new sponsorship model . . .' It disposed of the bad news in three convoluted sentences. By that time, every journalist in Britain had filed it under 'boring government puffery'. Then it covered its tracks, with a further mind-numbing 17 paragraphs of marketingspeak.

The disguise worked. Few people noticed, but it meant that sponsors will in future no longer put up any capital costs for academies at all. Instead, they are invited to make 'endowments' which the school can use at some later date.

This gave a special piquancy to Education Secretary Ruth Kelly's fatuous remark the previous year that we need business sponsors because 'business doesn't tolerate failure'. By then the search for business sponsors was self-evidently failing, and other sponsors – churches, charities, even the much-despised local authorities – were being dragged in to take their place.

There is a strong relationship between sponsors and the companies which make their profits out of privatizing services, like schools and hospitals. Sponsors often hire these companies to run academies, as 3Es was appointed to run Bexley Business Academy. And it is these latter companies, as the Register of Interests of MPs and Lords shows, which tend to complete the

slightly grubby circle by employing former ministers and officials as parliamentary advisers.

Take Lord Filkin, the man who wanted city academies to be
free of all that state bureaucracy, who was at the DfES from
September 2004 until May 2005 and has now returned to the
back benches. Some compensation for his new-found obscurity
comes from a directorship of Serco, which makes much of its
money by taking over the management of schools, and has
extensive interests in school privatization. It has a contract to
run Bradford's schools and education services. As it says on its
website, the company is 'one of the leading private sector
partners operating within the education and children's services
sectors'. Or take Charles Clarke, former Education Secretary,
now, among other things, a non-executive director of L.J.
Group, which is seeking work under the Government's Building
Schools for the Future programme, the main driver of the city
academy programme.

Sir Bruce Liddington, appointed in 2000 to give professional
advice to the DfES on academy projects, is also a freelance asso-
ciate for Veredus Executive Outsourcing, which was selected to
find senior staff, including heads, for three London academies,
the *TES* reported on 27 August 2004. Veredus is a part of the
Capita group whose founder and chairman, Rod Aldridge,
sponsored the academy in Blackburn. Sir Bruce, the *TES* added,
was also chairman of the East Midlands Leadership Centre,
which appointed Veredus to recruit its new commercial
director. However, he pointed out that he declared his interest
and took no part in the selection of Veredus. This does leave one
wondering why he is allowed private interests which may force
him to withhold his advice on key matters.

Some sponsors pulled out when they saw the strength of local
and national opposition, and the resentment they were creating.

Those who stayed the course often feel victimized and misunderstood by the media. 'It's a lot of hard work and you have the press continually doubting your motives,' says Steve Chalke of the Oasis Trust. And that, no doubt, is true, but is it really surprising?

Let's look at some of the sponsors.

Sir David Garrard

Who? Property developer behind Minerva. Knighted in 2003 for services to charity. Personally put forward by Tony Blair for peerage, but blocked by Lords appointment commission. Subsequently asked for name to be removed from No. 10's list. John Prescott gave the go-ahead to Minerva to build the controversial Park Place shopping centre in Croydon, which will become one of the country's ten biggest shopping malls, reversing a previous decision, some months after Garrard and his partner Andrew Rosenfeld had between them loaned Labour a total of £3.3 million.[3] Peter Kilfoyle, the former Labour Defence Minister, said this made the Government and the Labour Party look 'desperately seedy'.

What did he give? A secret loan to the Labour Party of £2.3 million in 2005, the biggest of the secret loans being investigated. He had already made the Party a gift of £200,000. His generosity also extended to the Conservative Party, which erected a plaque in his honour after he paid £70,000 to install a call centre at Conservative Central Office. Opened Bexley Business Academy in south London with £2.4 million sponsorship.

Barry Townsley CBE

Who? Chairman of stockbrokers Insinger Townsley. At centre of share-dealing scandal in the 1980s when he was barred from trading floor. CBE in 2004 for services to education and the arts. Recommended for peerage but blocked by the Lords appointment commission. Subsequently asked for name to be removed from list.

What did he give? A secret loan to the Labour Party of just over £1 million. A donation of £10,000 to Frank Dobson's campaign as Tony Blair's candidate to be the first Mayor of London against Ken Livingstone. Sponsored Stockley Academy, in Hillingdon, Middlesex. Pledged £1.5 million, but by May 2006 had only paid out £750,000.

Quote: 'I am delighted to be involved in giving young people the opportunity to develop skills at school that will help them gain jobs in tomorrow's employment market.'

Robert Edmiston

Who? His Birmingham-based IM Group made £14.6 million profit on £269 million sales in 2002, after Edmiston took £12 million salary. IM Group is one of Britain's biggest importers of cars from the Far East with franchises for Subaru, Isuzu and Daihatsu, and is valued at £200 million. An evangelical Christian, he has put £63 million into his Christian Vision charity, which broadcasts by satellite from Birmingham with on-air pastors, taking the Bible to developing countries. Nominated for a Tory life peerage by the former Conservative leader Michael Howard. Peerage blocked by the Lords appointment commission after an objection by the Inland Revenue.[4] Chose the name of his academy – Grace Academy – to reflect his evangelical Christianity.

What did he give? Tory party donor, funding Constituency Campaigning Services, a strategy centre charged with targeting 164 marginal seats. The Tories do not declare his money, which is a six-figure sum every year, claiming that CCS is officially independent of the party. Has provided £2 million sponsorship for the £31 million Grace Academy in Solihull, and is sponsoring a new academy to replace Woodway Park School in Coventry.

Quote: He has a 'traditional view of education', favouring a daily act of collective worship, Christian values and strong discipline. He is 'committed to bringing people into a relationship with Jesus' and has 'developed a number of global strategies to achieve this, including "Touch a Billion" and "Impact a Nation".'

Lord Laidlaw

Who? Set up International Institute for Research in 1992 – now a multinational business producing specialist newsletters and organizing conferences, employing 2,000 people in 28 countries. Until recently, a tax exile in Monaco. Has an estimated personal fortune of between £200 million and £700 million and, according to the *Sunday Times* rich list, he is the sixth wealthiest person in Scotland. Tory life peer in 2004 on recommendation of former Tory leader Iain Duncan Smith.

What did he give? A major donor to the Conservative Party. According to *The Scotsman*, he 'almost single-handedly bankrolls the Scottish Conservative Party'. Sponsor for an academy in Newcastle upon Tyne which will replace West Gate Community College in September 2008.

Quote: asked if he would stop funding the Scottish Conservative Party if it backed fiscal autonomy, under which the Scottish Parliament would raise its own revenue, he said: 'Scotland has a fantastic deal at the moment and we would be daft to change that. I would have to seriously reconsider my support.' Those backing the policy 'should keep their mouths shut if they have got any sense'.

Sir Clive Bourne

Who? Life president of Seabourne Group PLC. Knighted in 2005 for services to charity and education.

What did he give? Pledged £2 million to Mossbourne Community Academy, Hackney, east London.

Sir Frank Lowe

Who? Founder of advertising agency. Knighted in 2001 for services to advertising industry and charitable work.

What did he give? £2 million to Capital City Academy, Willesden, London.

Sir Peter Vardy

Who? Evangelical Christian who has built his father's car dealership, Reg Vardy plc, up from a single showroom, which he took over aged just 29 in 1976, to 98 dealerships located around the country, with 6,000 employees and an annual turnover of £1.7 billion. He is a close friend of Tony Blair, and was knighted in 2001 for services to business and education in north-east England.

What did he give? His Emmanuel Schools Foundation controls two academies, King's Academy in Middlesbrough and Trinity Academy in Thorne and Moorends, Doncaster, both of which he has sponsored for £2 million. Sir Peter was the first person to come forward and offer money for city academies when David Blunkett announced the scheme in 2000, and had already sponsored a CTC.

Quote: 'Who started education? It was the churches that started education'.[5] Nigel McQuoid, head of the Emmanuel Schools Foundation, claims that to say they teach creationism is simplistic and wrong, but he said in a lecture to the Christian Institute, 1997:

To teach children that they are developed mutations who evolved from something akin to a monkey as a result of a cataclysmic chemical accident and that death is the end of everything is hardly going to engender within them a sense of purpose, self-worth and respect. To present, however, the Truth that they were made by a loving and just God who sees every one of them as being of equal and real value and capable of achieving their best, and to speak of the life beyond death, creates an altogether more positive sense of responsibility, accountability and direction.

Roger de Haan CBE

Who? Chairman of Saga, Kent-based company which sells holidays for older people. CBE in 2004 for services to business, charity and education. Believes he will get a better, more willing workforce for his Kent-based business from an academy specializing in entrepreneurship.

What did he give? £1 million towards cost of academy in Ramsgate, Kent. May (or may not) be one-half of sponsorship of academy in Sheppey, with Kent County Council (see Chapter 4).

Quote: 'Businesses want more "work-ready", enterprising people . . . The Ramsgate Academy will embrace and wholeheartedly address the business needs identified by investing in pupils, ensuring that every child will get at least five days of enterprise education.'

John Madejski OBE

Who? Chairman of Reading Football Club. OBE in 2000 for contribution to Reading FC and local community. The John Madejski Academy will join other monuments to his wealth: the John Madejksi Garden at the Victoria and Albert Museum, the John Madejski Centre for Reputation at Henley Management College.

What did he give? Sponsor of the John Madejski Academy in Reading.

Quote: 'The academy goes back to an invitation I had to 10 Downing Street when [Charles] Clarke was Education Secretary. They had quite a few entrepreneurs and businessmen there. They wanted me to get involved in launching an academy in London. I was very attracted to the scheme, but wasn't interested in London'.[6]

Jack Petchey OBE

Who? Made a fortune as car salesman and property developer. The Petchey group now handles property investment and development, and timeshare management. OBE in 2004 for services to young people in east London and Essex. The home page of the academy website is dominated by a special offer for Mr Petchey's autobiography, which describes the sponsor thus:

> Jack Petchey – self-made millionaire – tells how he struggled as a young boy in school, started working at a young age, spent the war years as a messenger boy and in the Fleet Air Arm; then, after having been discouraged by the words 'You're not management material!' proved the world wrong by going from financial strength to strength, and finally giving it all back to young people in London, Essex and Portugal. A modern-day tale of rags to riches!

What did he give? Sponsor of the Jack Petchey Academy, Hackney, London, which opened in September 2006.

Quote: 'In a real "rags to riches" story, Jack Petchey rose from office boy at 14 in the accounts department of a legal stationers in the City of London to motor trade and property tycoon. The years following World War II saw the birth of the Petchey Group, with Jack Petchey rapidly escalating from owning and driving a minicab, to controlling a fleet of hire cars, then opening car showrooms, and subsequently diversifying to purchasing properties including the development of the immensely popular Clube Praia da Oura in the Algarve, Portugal.'[7]

Lord Harris of Peckham

Who? Made a fortune selling carpets. An early supporter of Margaret Thatcher for Tory Party leader, then of William Hague, then an early supporter of David Cameron. Made a Tory life peer in 1995, before academy programme but after CTC programme. All his academies are called Harris Academy.

What did he give? A former Conservative Party treasurer. Sponsor of five academies in London at Peckham, Southwark, Bermondsey, Merton and East Dulwich. Was previously a sponsor of city technology colleges.

Quote: 'I was a great backer of [William] Hague. I think he would have done very, very well. The mistake I made was bringing him on too early. It wouldn't have mattered who went up against Blair in those first four years, no one was going to make an impression. Hague was five years too early. [David] Cameron thinks about people. I think about people.'

Sir Harry Djanogly

Who? Nottingham textile mogul, chairman of Coats Viyella. Knighthood 1993 (before academies but after CTCs).

What did he give? Sponsor of Djanogly City Academy, Nottingham. But he gave it no money at all, on the grounds that he had sponsored its predecessor, the Djanogly CTC.

Quote: when his company, Coats Viyella, announced 2,000 job losses: 'We have determined to invest only in those businesses capable of delivering profitable growth, and to sell or close the rest.'

Absolute Return for Kids
What? A charity set up by very wealthy people in the hedge fund business, the inspiration of Arpad 'Arki' Busson, French multimillionaire financier and father of Elle Macpherson's two children. Its director of education, Jay Altman, came from the USA in 2005. Altman was the founding principal of the New Orleans charter middle school in Louisiana. It also hired Sally Morgan when she left her post as Blair's chief of staff.

What did it give? Planned to set up a network of seven academies, on the US charter school model. But withdrew from first project, the planned academy in Islington. It has one open academy, in White City, west London, and plans for three more, all in London.

Rod Aldridge OBE
Who? Founder and former executive chairman of services firm Capita, whose business is mostly government and public service contracts. It is expected to make £200 million in 2006. Among other contracts, it collects the television licence fee, administers London's congestion charge, runs large parts of the BBC's personnel department, and operates the DfES numeracy and literacy strategies. It also runs the Home Office Criminal Records Bureau, which descended into chaos. He was warned of a potential conflict of interest because Capita won the £190 million 15-year contract with Blackburn and Darwen Council to support regeneration in 2001. The DfES Academies Unit told him the Government was keen to involve Mr Aldridge as a

sponsor but 'there were difficulties in his sponsoring an academy in the area because of his relationship with the council'. However, ministers overruled this objection and agreed to the sponsorship. Capita is New Labour's favourite public sector contractor, though it has been widely criticized for its performance on several Government contracts and is colloquially known as 'Crapita', a name invented by *Private Eye* magazine. It has a contract to manage the government's strategy for improving literacy and numeracy in schools. Aldridge's OBE dates from 1994. He resigned as chairman of Capita in March 2006, after his Labour Party loan was made public, to avoid speculation that his support for the academy might be linked to the estimated £3 billion Capita has made from Government contracts in the last nine years.

What did he give? Secretly lent £1 million to the Labour Party, a loan which is being investigated by the police. Pledged £2 million to an academy in Blackburn via his personal charitable trust. His £35 million academy is to specialize in entrepreneurship, and 150 homes are being knocked down to build it.

Quote: 'There have been suggestions that this loan [to the Labour Party] has resulted in the group being awarded government contracts. This is entirely spurious.'[8]

United Learning Trust
What? Christian educational charity created to found academies. Its parent organization is the United Church Schools Trust, which runs ten private fee-charging schools with over 7,000 pupils. It is run by a board of 19 members, ten of whom are appointed by the UCST. The ULT is ultimately responsible for, and is the legal employer and admissions authority for each of its academies. It is chaired by Dame Angela Rumbold and the chief executive is Sir Ewan Harper. UCST's chairman is Lord

Carey, former Archbishop of Canterbury. It raises the money for its schools from business. Its eight fee-charging schools will benefit from the public investment in its academies: ULT intends its fee-charging schools and its academies to 'work together to cross private and public sector educational boundaries in a unique way'. Sir Ewan Harper told the *Guardian* that his charity had raised more than £15 million without a single donor hinting at receiving an honour. However, Sir Ewan was knighted in 2003 for services to the Church of England, on the recommendation of former Archbishop of Canterbury George Carey. The ULT trustees will run all the ULT's academies, and they are said to keep a tight grip on all decision-making about them.

What did it give? Eight academies running, with plans to sponsor 20. The biggest academy sponsor, it already controls the education of more children than several local education authorities. For its first three academies it paid the full sponsorship of £2 million, but then took advantage of the Government's special offer and is paying £1.5 million each for the rest. In Manchester it is only putting up £575,000 as it is a joint sponsor. It came in 'as a result of dialogue with the Government'.

Quote: 'We are at one of those seminal moments in history where significant change is occurring: independent schools are being introduced into the state sector on a scale that has never been seen before. Do we want to be part of it, or are we going to let the moment slip past?' (Sir Ewan Harper, chief executive). Its publicity says: 'The Christian faith will be the starting point and central focus for the ethos of the Trust and the academy.' It also says: 'As a sponsor, ULT would be responsible for the appointment of a majority of governors, who with their colleagues would be responsible for the appointment of staff, all curriculum detail within the overall framework of the National Curriculum, the choice of specialism and governance.'

Oasis

What? A Christian trust founded by Steve Chalke MBE. It campaigns for faith organizations to be allowed to employ only people of their own religion, and gives advice on how to avoid laws which prevent discrimination against homosexuals, according to the NUT's pamphlet *Academies: Looking Beyond the Spin*. Its funding comes from Government, local authorities, donors and supporters. Mr Chalke is an evangelical Christian, a Baptist minister who has caused a split in the evangelical ranks. He started Oasis in 1985, and in 1996 he founded Oasis Media, which calls itself 'an integrated communications agency providing PR, internet and production solutions to clients in the charity/social responsibility sector'. In 2000 he founded xalt.co.uk, a website consisting of simple religious homilies, quotations from the Bible, and advertisements for religious books. Steve Chalke's MBE was awarded in 2004 for services to inclusion. His charity does a great deal more than just sponsor academies. All its academies are to be called The Oasis Academy.

What did it give? Academy in Enfield to open September 2007, and four more to follow in Grimsby, Immingham, Bristol and Salford. Paid £2 million for the first three, and £1.5 million thereafter. Mr Chalke claims that they spend more than this in reality, so as to ensure that Oasis academies also provide community services. Money for academies comes from 'people who have trusted us in the past', some of them giving specifically for the academy, and some giving generally to Oasis.

Quote: Oasis academies 'will be rooted in Christian-based core values, which it is hoped will permeate every aspect of its life'.

The Haberdashers Company

What? The Worshipful Company of Haberdashers has its origins in medieval times. In six-and-a-half centuries it has moved away from its involvement in the trade of haberdashery and involves itself in schools and education in England and Wales. It runs private, fee-charging schools as well as state schools.

What did it give? Has pledged just £295,000 to two academies in Lewisham, south London, leaving taxpayer to pick up the rest of the £38 million bill. By May 2006 had not paid anything.

Quote: 'Haberdasher schools encourage the full development of individuals, and help them to get the most out of their work and leisure time. They promote a broad tolerance of different viewpoints and consideration of others, within the context of a Christian heritage.'

The Church of England

What? The established Church.

What did it give? Academies in Merton, Haringey, Bradford, Leeds and Leicester.

Quote: 'It's about front-line evangelism' says church commissioner Peter Bruinvels.[9]

The Roman Catholic Church

What? The Latin Church.

What did it give? Academies in Greenwich, Lewisham and Liverpool.

Quote: 'We expect only that we will be able to continue to give first preference to Catholic children when our school places are insufficient in number to meet the demand from all . . . We will robustly oppose any steps to introduce quotas for non-faith places in our schools'.[10]

Amey PLC
What? One of the UK's leading providers of outsourced services, with a 1999 turnover of £523 million. Amey is currently involved in the £1.2 billion programme to modernize many of Glasgow's secondary schools, and provides services to around 500 other education establishments.

What did it give? Sponsor of Unity City Academy, East Middlesbrough.

Peter Shalson
Who? Chairman of SGI Ltd, venture capitalist. According to the *Sunday Times* rich list, he 'transformed Braitrim, a coat hanger supplier, into a packaging business which he sold for £109 million. The sale of Brightview, an internet company, netted him a further £25 million. He moved into pubs, and the £162.5 million purchase of 545 pubs from Punch Taverns last December has brought his Pubfolio chain to more than 800 pubs valued at £250 million before tax. He has other interests.'

What did he give? Sponsors the London Academy, specializing in business and IT, with £1.5 million.

Quote: 'There is a great entrepreneurial spirit in the school. There is a very large proportion of ethnic minorities and they are traditionally entrepreneurs. I want to harness that.'

*   *   *

As commercial sponsors became harder to get, and the churches reached their limits, some public bodies started to come into the scheme – using public, not private, money.

Public bodies acting as sponsors include the University of the West of England (one of two sponsors of City Academy, Bristol); City University (one of two sponsors of proposed academy in Islington); the Corporation of London (sponsor of City of London Academy, Southwark, and one of two sponsors of a proposed academy in Islington); Kent County Council (one half of sponsorship of an academy on the Isle of Sheppey, Kent); and Liverpool University (half sponsorship of North Liverpool Academy).

Some CTCs – which are, of course, publicly owned but privately run, like academies – are becoming the 'sponsor' of their own academy.

Very small players include a fifth of the sponsorship of Sandwell Academy each for HSBC, West Bromwich Albion Football Club, and Tarmac; half sponsorship of North Liverpool Academy for Granada Learning; and part sponsorship of Harefield Academy in Hillingdon by David Meller.

Notes

1. Richard Hatcher, *Privatization and Sponsorship: The Re-agenting of the School System in England*, 2006.
2. *Sunday Times*, 16 and 21 April 2006.
3. *Daily Telegraph*, 23 March 2006.
4. *Guardian*, 3 October 2006.
5. BBC Radio 4, 11 March 2002.
6. Richard Garner, *Independent*, 5 September 2006.
7. From the home page of the Petchey Group.
8. *Evening Standard*, 20 July 2006.
9. Quoted in *The Academies: Looking Beyond the Spin*, National Union of Teachers.
10. Catholic Education Service.

4

How They Tore Up the Laws on Schools

There is a whole body of law governing state schools, providing rights for parents and pupils, and ensuring that the state and the schools have certain duties towards them. The law has been built up over six decades since the landmark 1944 Education Act which provided for free education for all young people. If a school is oversubscribed, it must follow procedures designed to ensure as much fairness as possible in admissions. If a school wants to exclude your child for any reason, it must follow certain procedures designed to ensure fairness, and your local authority must find a way of giving your child an education. And so on.

Not a single paragraph of any of these laws or procedures applies to city academies. They are not state schools, and they are above all the laws applying to state schools.

In the place of these laws, each academy has a funding agreement. If a parent or pupil wants to complain of unfair treatment, they cannot look to the law: they have to look to the funding agreement. And that may be entirely useless to them, because it is not at all clear that a parent or a pupil can ask a court to enforce a funding agreement. We do not yet know for certain; it depends on how the courts interpret the law. But parents and pupils are not parties to funding agreements, which are negotiated between the sponsor and the Government. No parent or pupil has yet tried to enforce one, but when they do, it is perfectly possible that the courts will rule that they have no standing, since they are not parties to it. One academy, Haber-dashers Knights Academy in Lewisham, south London, has already claimed that parents cannot enforce the funding agreement.

And even if they can enforce them, the best of these agreements give parents and pupils substantially fewer rights than the law gives them in state schools. The worst of them – the earliest ones, which were based on those for the city technology colleges – give parents and pupils virtually no rights at all.

The Government has drawn up a model funding agreement, but this is open to negotiation if a sponsor wants to change it. And the funding agreements are frozen at the time they are negotiated. If, in ordinary state schools, we wish parents and pupils to have greater rights, we can campaign for a change in the law. But a campaign will do us no good in city academies, for a funding agreement can only be changed with the agreement of the sponsor.

The law relating to excluding children, for example, changes frequently. These changes will not be reflected at academies. This, we already know, results in a far less sympathetic method of dealing with exclusions at academies. Local authorities have built up over the years a system of 'managed transfers' which allows children who cannot be kept on in one school to be given a fresh start in another. But this requires all the schools in a given area to co-operate, and academies are under no obligation to co-operate.

Schools are required to begin with a fixed-term three-day exclusion, then take the pupil back. In at least one academy, children are told that if they do return, they will be permanently excluded. This is effectively permanent exclusion, and is illegal in state schools. It means that the academy's permanent exclusion rates look lower than they really are. It also means the pupils are in limbo. They have not, in theory, been excluded, so cannot claim a legal right to a place somewhere else, but they cannot go back to their school. It undermines the idea that all children should be given an education, and a growing number of children will grow up without the knowledge and skills to earn any sort of living. These are the children who will, in future, swell our prison population.

Pupils in state schools can appeal to an independent panel against their exclusion. In an academy, the funding agreement normally states that the panel is appointed by the school itself. In some cases, it is the academy's governing body, on which the sponsor has an inbuilt majority. In at least two academies – the two run by the Haberdashers Company – there is no right to appeal to an independent body, as there has to be in state schools.

Admissions policies vary from agreement to agreement. Religious education policies can generally be unilaterally amended by the governing body, on which, in academies, the sponsor always has an inbuilt majority. The model funding agreement gives parents and children the same rights in relation to religious education as they have in state schools. But several city academies, notably the religious ones, have altered it to give parents and children fewer rights and the school greater powers. Take, for example, the statutory right which state school parents have to withdraw their children from religious education. Some funding agreements do not give academy parents this right.

Barrister David Wolfe (see below) says that in some academies 'the funding agreement appears to allow for religious elements to extend far beyond the RE and collective worship aspects of school life, such that any right to withdraw may be extremely difficult to exercise in practice.' The Bexley City Academy funding agreement gives the right to withdraw from religious education, but adds that cross-curricular learning of religious education will be taught through English and cultural studies as well as science, geography, history, dance and drama.

A *Times Educational Supplement* analysis of funding agreements in February 2006 showed that 12 of what were then 27 academies – nearly half of them – were using their power to select 10 per cent of their intake by 'aptitude'.

Academies can exempt themselves, through the negotiations over the funding agreement, from the requirement to take a child with special educational needs who has a statement naming the school.

Parents and local council taxpayers get little or no chance to comment on the funding agreement before it is signed, sealed and delivered. The only statutory requirement is that the Government must consult the local authority. A good local authority may choose to consult local parents, though the consultation is generally perfunctory, for the local authority, as we have seen, is under enormous financial pressure to agree city academy proposals.

Control of education is being taken out of the hands of voters, parents and pupils and placed in the hands of a few self-selected sponsors, and six decades of schools legislation and case law are being casually junked. That's how two campaigning lawyers, solicitor Richard Stein of Leigh, Day, and barrister David Wolfe of Matrix Chambers, saw it. 'The funding agreement is a contract which is secretive,' says Wolfe.

They also saw that there was a way in which it could be challenged through the courts. The first phase of the establishment of a city academy is to decide to close an existing school, or several existing schools, in order to make way for it. If that decision is made when the final detail of the funding agreement is still not known, then the council which takes the decision does not really know what it is doing, and neither do the parents and the governors of the school or schools to be closed. Stein and Wolfe believe you could argue in law that it had no right to take a decision until it understood the nature of the decision it was taking.

In 2006 some parents came forward as litigants over the establishment of academies in Merton, Islington and the Isle of Sheppey, and Stein and Wolfe acted for them. The story of those cases is instructive, and offers disturbing evidence about the lengths to which politicians will go to force an unwanted idea on people.

Merton

In recent years Merton's education authority has conducted a radical reorganization. It changed from a three-tier system to the more normal two-tier system in which pupils go to secondary school at age 11, and it took the sixth forms out of the secondary schools and put them into colleges. As a result, by 2005 Merton had eight secondary schools. Two of these were Roman Catholic. One of the remaining six was a voluntary aided school, Rutlish, which found its way into the media spotlight in the 1990s as the school once attended by John Major. They all taught 11–16-year-olds.

Of the five others, the council proposed in 2005 that two, Tamworth Manor and Mitcham Vale, should become city academies. The reorganization meant that the council had spent significant sums of money on the two schools, especially Mitcham Vale which had merged with another school only two years previously. They spent the money in the only way the Government would allow them to spend it – by a Private Finance Initiative (PFI) contract with New Schools (Merton)

Ltd, a front for construction giant Atkins Asset Management. The company had a 25-year contract to build and manage the schools. It meant that the schools resembled building sites for some years, which decreased their popularity. Mitcham Vale was just coming out of special measures.

The academy to replace Mitcham Vale had as its sponsors the charity Toc H, the Church of England (Southwark diocese) and the education consultancy CFBT. It was to become Merton Church of England Academy and was to specialize in health and social care. Tamworth Manor's sponsor was to be Lord Harris, the carpet magnate, and it was to specialize in sport.

Mitcham Vale, which had been a non-denominational school welcoming pupils of any religion or none, was to be permitted to select up to one-third of its pupils on the basis of church attendance. Its admissions policy refers to 'children whose families are faithful and regular worshippers in an Anglican church'. At Lord Harris's school, according to his proposal, 'the ethos of the academy will reflect an enterprise culture, involving the explicit development of business knowledge and skills'.

The sponsors told the council that they wanted to be free to manage their schools as they chose, and would not therefore take them on if they were encumbered with a PFI contract. If a local authority said the same thing, the Government would simply prevent it from spending the money. But since sponsors were saying it, a way had to be found to meet their wishes.

But Atkins Asset Management had a clause in their contract which meant that the local authority had to pay them if it withdrew any schools from the contract. So the council (perhaps – we do not know for certain – with help from the Government) paid off Atkins Asset Management.

We do now know how much taxpayers' money had to be handed over. The information is 'commercial in confidence'.

We do know that it was a very large sum. Atkins had to be compensated for their capital spending at the two schools. They also had to be compensated for 'loss of future profits' from managing the two schools for the next 25 years. In a paper for councillors, Dave Hill, the council's director of children, schools and families, estimated the loss of future profits payment would be between £800,000 and £1.2 million. 'In addition', wrote Mr Hill, 'there would be other associated expenses legitimately incurred in bringing about the partial termination.' This means lawyers, management consultants, that sort of thing, and almost certainly runs into hundreds of thousands of pounds.

Altogether, then, the council had to pay out millions of pounds to deliver these schools to the sponsors unencumbered by a PFI contract. And they did it in a hurry, because Mr Hill warned them that, if they delayed, for example to allow more public consultation, they would be hit with an even bigger bill. 'This would result in the PFI contractor having to reassess, at some expense, termination costs in conjunction with subcontractors and others. These assessment charges will be payable by Merton.'

It is an odd irony that the Government forces PFI contracts onto councils, to place them in the hands of a private company, and tells us how good PFI contracts are. But when they hand the whole school, lock, stock and barrel, over to a private company, that company will only take it if the PFI contract is junked. It will come as no surprise to anyone who has studied PFI contracts that the private sector considers them a bad deal for everyone except the contractor.

Both schools wanted to have sixth forms, a request which was immediately granted even though it made nonsense of the whole reorganization upon which the council had spent so much time and money. Consultation with local parents was rushed and perfunctory, and was over in just five weeks. Nonetheless, protesters can work fast if they feel strongly enough about it. A campaign group was set up swiftly to oppose the academies, and a parent went to Richard Stein to make a demand for a judicial review.

The New Labour spin machine swung swiftly into action to denigrate the characters of everyone who opposed the project. It came, I think, as rather a shock to the perhaps naive campaigners to find just how brutal, personal, vindictive and dishonest the black propaganda was. The Government was determined to open the new academies in September 2006, and to do this it needed to crush the campaign in a matter of weeks.

The parent who called for a judicial review, Rob MacDonald, found himself the subject of a secret New Labour investigation. He, the spinners discovered, was a member of the Socialist Party, and long extracts from this party's leaflets appeared in the local authority's statements to the court. They were, of course, irrelevant to the legal issues, but no doubt they were judged to serve the purpose of publicly discrediting Mr MacDonald.

I prefer to take Mr MacDonald at his own estimate. He says he did not want to see the closure of a school which had served his son and other children rather well. His son had had some difficulty at school:

The teachers had put an awful lot of effort with my son to turn things round and together they are succeeding. Just before its proposed closure, the school delivered a set of GCSE results that showed it to be the most improved school in the borough. It has become a good local comprehensive school and the last thing my son needed was for his school to be closed and suddenly transformed into something else entirely in his GCSE year. The head had recently been given an award by the Mayor of London and Lord Adonis himself for running the most improved school in the area.

The local MP, Siobhain McDonagh, a New Labour loyalist, said the campaign was run by sacked school governors. A whole governing body had been sacked a few years previously, but the campaign was in fact run by Audrey King, who had been governor of Tamworth Manor School for 16 years and had never been sacked. Ms McDonagh said they were failing schools, but one was coping reasonably well and improving fast, while the other had come out of special measures. Ms McDonagh also sent to parents a questionnaire. It was one of those questionnaires in which New Labour's least principled spinners specialize. Each question had a box which you could either tick or cross, and it went like this:

☐ Yes, I am in favour of raising standards at Mitcham Vale and Tamworth Manor High School by getting academy status.

☐ No, I am against these changes to Mitcham Vale and Tamworth Manor High Schools designed to improve examination results.

Either you are in favour of academy status *and* raising standards; or you are against academy status, *and* you want low standards. She wrote to residents: 'I've heard a lot of scare stories so I want to reassure you here and now both schools will continue to be open to local children, free and owned by the local community.' In fact, an academy is not owned by the local community but by the sponsor, and how 'open to local children' Merton Church of England Academy is depends on whether those local children regularly worship at an Anglican church.

Despite these tactics, when the council did send out 1,500 letters with a tearoff slip to ask whether parents approved the idea of the academies, the vote was four to one against. Just 21 people voted in favour. At each of the three public meetings, it was obvious that most people opposed the academy proposals.

'In contrast,' reported Dave Hill to the council, 'the feedback received from Siobhain McDonagh's consultation was overwhelmingly supportive of the proposals.' However, added Mr Hill dryly, 'some respondents to the Council's consultation criticized the wording of the questions asked by Ms McDonagh'. People are not as stupid as politicians like Siobhain McDonagh think they are.

The consultation was done so fast that by the time Mr MacDonald's request for judicial review of the decision to close the two schools came to court, there was only a month to go. It was July, and at the end of August the schools were to become academies.

His lawyers argued that there had been no proper consultation, that those consulted were not able to see the actual or likely funding agreement, and that neither was the council. But Mr MacDonald's petition for judicial review was rejected. As the campaign group reported afterwards: 'The judgement by the high court on 27th July was a defeat on a legal technicality and has not tested our claim that Merton council consultation to parents and the community was flawed.' The legal technicality was that, in order to save time, the action was brought against the schools adjudicator who accepted the council's verdict. The group added: 'The very nature of the rushed consultation and the possible negative impact on the schools was the major reason for this ruling and our lack of being prompt in developing the case against the adjudicator. As the judge himself stated in his summing up, it was "simply too late".'

The schools closed on 31 August 2006, and the academies opened the next day.

Islington

The same month as the Merton hearing came to court, another court was deciding whether to allow a popular primary school to be closed in order to make way for a much larger 'through' academy for 4- to 16-year-olds in Islington, north London. This was to be one of two academies in Islington – the story of the other is told in Chapter 7.

St Mary Magdalene, the primary school due to be closed, had a recent Ofsted inspection which described it as 'a very good school' and added: 'Most groups of pupils achieve very well because teaching, learning and the curriculum are very good overall. SEN [special needs] pupils achieve exceptionally well.' Parents, it said, prized the fact that it was small and friendly, and their children were safe, happy and learning. There ought to be a very, very good reason before you consider closing a school like that.

Nonetheless, the proposal, published in February 2005, was to close the school, and open St Mary Magdalene Academy on the site in September 2007.

Hayley Powers, who had two children at the school, asked for a judicial review of the decision. She claimed that the council and the Office for the Schools Adjudicator, which approved the closure, failed to take into account the fact that children's human rights would be undermined, because the safeguards granted to pupils at state schools would be lost.

Her barrister, David Wolfe, says: 'Parents were being told: forgo your rights in maintained schools, in favour of something about which you only have a glossy brochure.' Those who asked for more information were referred to the model funding agreement on the DfES website, but this is only a model and 'it changes every time we fight a case. In Islington, as in Merton, parents were being asked to agree to the statutory closure of the existing school, when they had no idea what kind of new school they would get without seeing the funding agreement, which was to come out later.'

Her solicitor Richard Stein gave a statement to the court. He said that the purpose of academies had been defined as 'to improve standards of education for pupils who have to date been failed'. Stein said:

> If that is indeed the primary purpose of the academies programme, it is difficult to see how it is fulfilled in this instance . . . It is clear that the primary school pupils here have not 'to date been failed' by the education system. In particular, the school being closed here to make way for the new academy is recognized to be a good school, placed higher than the national average in the performance league table, and given a 'very good' rating in its last Ofsted inspection.

Currently parents constituted one-third of the governors, he said; they would probably be reduced to one, and there would be an inbuilt majority for the sponsor. There would be no external complaints procedure. The school would not have the same obligation to take special needs children, an area where the primary school excelled. There would be no external appeal panel on exclusions. The right of parents to withdraw children from religious education was in danger. There might be no means of enforcing even the diminished rights in the funding agreement.

Parents who wanted to know what was on offer were told to

look at the model funding agreement, he said. But for a time it was not available on the DfES website. 'It is certainly not clear what comfort parents and others are expected to draw from a document which, even if it were to be made available to them, is clearly apt to change during the process.'

St Mary Magdalene having served special needs children especially well, Stein thought it worthwhile drawing the court's attention to the fact that several previous academies had been able to negotiate funding agreements which made it hard for special needs children to get in. In particular, the Haberdashers academies only gave priority to special needs children if the school itself had agreed to be named in their statement. This is a far worse deal than they get in state schools. Might not the same happen in Islington?

Parents and children were likely to have far fewer rights – in admissions, in exclusions, in representation on the governing body, in pretty well everything, Stein argued. The DfES replied that they had already put a lot of money into building – the academy proposal was well advanced by then – and all this money would be wasted if the academy decision was crushed.

Now, this is a very odd argument indeed. As Stein put it: 'If there is a need for a new state-funded school in the area, then the claimants are not in principle opposed to such a school being built . . . There is nothing inherent in the building which is being built that says that the school in question must be an academy. It could just as well be a maintained school (or schools – a separate primary and secondary school).' This would 'allow for what should have happened in the first place, namely proper consideration of whether the new school should be a maintained school or an academy'.

Of course, there was never the slightest chance this would happen. If the Government is thwarted by parents in its pet scheme, its past history suggests that it will pursue a scorched-earth policy, leaving the area derelict and hoping that it will serve as a terrible warning to other areas considering fighting an academy proposal.

On 26 July 2006 Mr Justice Wilkie handed down his verdict. He had been reminded by the DfES of the Education Secretary's statutory guidance: that when it came to academies, 'there should be a general presumption in favour of approval'. And he concluded: 'I reject the contention that the maintained sector constitutes a gold standard and that any falling away from that standard requires justification, failing which approval for continuance should not flow.' The application for judicial review was dismissed.

The campaign group Residents Against the Mary Magdalene Academy commented:

> The academy is not replacing a failing secondary school, but a successful and popular primary school, whose perfectly good building is being torn down. The site is too small for the development, so that the playground is on the roof, lunch-times will be staggered over three hours, and some children will have to eat in their classrooms.
>
> The sixth form is unnecessary. City and Islington College, also expensive new-build, is in the top ten Ofsted-rated UK sixth-form colleges. Its intake may suffer as a direct result of the academy's sixth form. The other academy planned for Islington, at Islington Green School [discussed in a separate chapter], is also to have a sixth form.
>
> Islington's nine existing secondary schools are undersubscribed. Other sixth forms are being reduced in size.

As I write (October 2006), St Mary Magdalene primary school enters the final year of its life. Its children and teachers watch the new academy going up in the grounds as they work. Parents regret the loss of their small, friendly, successful school, and are not looking forward to sending their children to a vast new institution. But there is nothing at all they can do about it.

Isle of Sheppey

Parents on the Isle of Sheppey set up an action group in 2004, when they first heard about Kent County Council's plan to replace all 12 maintained schools – eight primary schools, three middle schools and one upper school – with one huge academy on several sites, catering for 3,500 pupils and costing £55 million. Since Sheppey is an island, connected to mainland Kent by a road-crossing, it would be the only school the children could reasonably get to. So much for the Government's professed determination to provide parental choice. At the same time the council wanted to reorganize the current three-tier system into two tiers.

In March 2006 the then Education Secretary, Ruth Kelly, approved an 'expression of interest' for the academy plans. And that is when parents discovered that something very odd had happened. They had been told that the sponsor was Roger de Haan, millionaire local businessman and founder of the Saga group, which organizes travel for older people. But the expression of interest named the sponsors as the Canterbury diocese of the Church of England, to provide 'leadership' of the academy board through the Bishop of Dover, Stephen Venner; and Kent County Council to provide the money (which was to be £1 million, not £2 million). The public school, Dulwich College, was to provide 'support in kind' worth £150,000, presumably in the form of advice on how to run a school, estimated on a generous hourly consultancy rate.

Having the local authority as sponsor goes against both the spirit and the letter of the law on city academies. Sponsors are supposed to be independent, and the whole idea was to take schools out of the dead hand of local government. So why did the Education Secretary suddenly decide that Kent was OK to be a sponsor?

Partly, no doubt, because there was no one else, Mr de Haan having decided not to part with any money after all. Partly, probably, because Kent is a sturdily Conservative council, pursuing traditional Conservative education policies such as selection by 11-plus examination. This may sound odd, since we have a Labour Government, and Ms Kelly was a Labour Education Secretary. But it is impossible to imagine her allowing, say, Labour Lambeth or Liberal Democrat Islington being the sponsor of their own academy.

If there is a case for inferior rights for parents and pupils in schools run by a private sponsor, there cannot be such a case in a school which is run by the local authority, and government funded, just like any other state school. It was no doubt in an attempt to answer this point that the DfES academies unit, which drew up the expression of interest, opted for the thin cover of saying that 'leadership' would come from the nearest bishop. 'I suspect this is the future of academies,' says David Wolfe. 'The peerages scandal has scared off most potential sponsors, and you will see the Kent model again.'

Wolfe's client in Sheppey was Robina Allum, whose seven children all attend Sheppey schools. She pointed out that once the expression of interest was agreed, the DfES handed over £250,000 to have a funding agreement prepared, so the approval had better be done properly. And she claimed that the

Education Secretary could not legally approve the expression of interest, because she did not know enough about it. For example, the expression of interest said that the governing body of Minster College supported the proposal, but in fact it had not been consulted.

She also claimed that having the local authority as sponsor was not in accordance with the law establishing city academies. They were supposed to be independent of local authorities, and they were supposed to bring in private money. Neither of these things could be said for an academy whose sponsorship money came entirely from the council.

Kent County Council frantically fudged this point. A press release in the same month as the expression of interest was approved said: 'A number of prominent sponsors from the business, charitable, church and independent school sector are partnering KCC in these proposals.' The fact was that there was only one sponsor in the proper sense – that is, actually putting up money – and that was Kent County Council. All the Bishop of Dover was called upon to do was to chair the academy board. And Dulwich College did not intend to contribute a single penny: its contribution is 'in kind', presumably in the form of advice.

By May, two months after the expression of interest, the academies unit at the DfES was claiming that Roger de Haan was back in the frame, and willing to put in £1 million. Robina Allum was therefore able to say that, if current information coming from the academies unit was correct, Ruth Kelly had approved the expression of interest on the basis of entirely false information. Ms Kelly thought Kent County Council was the only sponsor putting in money, but Mr de Haan was to put in money; she thought the Bishop of Dover was to chair the board, but he was not; she thought Minster College governors knew and approved, but they did not.

When I looked at the DfES website in October, the Bishop had disappeared. His office confirms that he is still interested, and would like to stamp the mark of Christianity over the new academy, but will neither contribute money nor chair the governing body.

It looks as though the DfES has had as much trouble finding out what is going on as I had. Halfway through the case, the Secretary of State gave Richard Stein a witness statement containing information that they had previously refused to give him, and which meant that Stein could no longer continue with the case. Since the DfES had failed to provide it at the proper time, it agreed to pay all the other side's costs – another few thousand pounds of the education budget wasted.

5

Faith in Academies

The Christian churches, with falling attendances and a crisis of confidence, have grabbed the chance massively to increase their importance in British education. The city academy programme is making Christian churches vastly more powerful in education – and cutting out other faiths, as well as secular schools. Of the 46 academies open as I write, 14 academies – just under one-third of the total – will be entirely in the control of Christian organizations or evangelical Christians. Three others have Christian organizations as one-half of the sponsorship team. All, in different ways, say that the faith is a central part of their academy, as do several others not overtly controlled by Christian organizations. These organizations will have the power to decide what is taught and how it is taught. No city academy has been founded by any non-Christian faith, though a Muslim academy is being mooted for Bradford.

This is a huge leap in the control Christianity has had on our education system. No one has ever tried to persuade us of the merits of handing huge swathes of our schools over to the Christian religion. There may be arguments for it, but no one has bothered to make those arguments. It has been done by stealth, by a Prime Minister who is himself a very religious man and a supporter of faith schools; but who, as the polls show, would not have been able to persuade the electorate that it was a good thing to do, if he had chosen to do it openly.

For 60 years, until the academy programme came along, a

careful compromise between Church and state had more or less held. The 1944 Education Act, which provided for universal state education, gave Christianity its place in the new system – a place which recognized that Britain is a Christian country, but also that a large and growing number of Britons are not Christians, and their views also need to be taken into account.

It was a compromise which does not satisfy all Christians, and sometimes seems to secular thinkers to undermine social cohesion. But it held, until the arrival of the Blair Government, led by a Prime Minister whose Christianity was more to the fore in his politics than any Prime Minister since Lord Salisbury left office in 1902. The Blair Government's frequent assertions that faith schools were somehow superior to other schools alarmed many people. In August 2005 a *Guardian*/ICM poll found that almost two-thirds of the public oppose ministers' plans to increase the number of religious schools.

But with the academies programme, the Blair Government can wash its hands of any such consensus. If the Christian churches want to use it to increase their presence and influence in education, they can do so. Many of the academy sponsors would like to put the clock back to the time when churches controlled education, and have seen that this is their chance to do so.

Of these sponsors, the two most disturbing ones are the evangelical Christians Sir Peter Vardy and Robert Edmiston.

*   *   *

Gordon Potter, former deputy head at Coulby Newham School in Middlesbrough, one of two schools closed in 2003 to make way for a city academy, is sick of reading about what a rotten school he used to help run. In an interview with a local news-

paper, King's Academy head teacher Nigel McQuoid claims
that Coulby Newham 'replaced two failing schools . . . (and)
inherited 1,000 pupils and 130 staff from failing schools – and
all the baggage that came with them'.[1]

This was not true. Mr Potter is justly proud of his old school,
into which he put the best years of his professional life. 'We had
six times the national average of special needs pupils and 35 per
cent of pupils eligible for free school meals. But we had the best
Key Stage 3 results in Middlesbrough in 2002', he says.

That year, the standards watchdog Ofsted praised Coulby
Newham School: 'The school provided a good quality of education, a good climate for learning, and good management and
efficiency.' Standards were improving; the school was successfully raising pupils' attainment; teaching was of high quality;
pupils were keen to learn, and difficult behaviour was well
managed. 'The contented frame of mind which predominates
in the school is a major achievement, given the statistical data
about the school and its intake. The school's leadership and
management are good.'

But the inspectors knew that Coulby Newham was doomed,
so they recommended that the new city academy should learn
from how the school did things. It did not do so. Some of the
things Coulby Newham did well, King's Academy does badly or
not at all; and its spokespeople persistently peddle the myth that
Coulby Newham failed. Not one member of the Coulby
Newham management team was appointed at King's Academy.

The other school, Brackenhoe, was not doing as well as
Coulby Newham, and had poor examination results. It was not
failing, though it may have been struggling.

But, as Jim Callaghan once said, a lie can be halfway round
the world before the truth has got its boots on. '[King's
Academy] replaced two failing schools in the south of the city'

reported local newspaper *The Journal* in February 2005, two years after its opening. This has become the general, and quite false, perception of what happened.

One of the minor sins to be laid at the door of academies is the stupid waste of talented, experienced, dedicated teachers. Mr Potter, like his head teacher, found himself distinctly unwelcome at the city academy, and was persuaded to take early retirement. He would have liked to have gone on teaching. He is forbidden, by terms of his agreement, to discuss his redundancy or King's Academy, and could only talk to me about Coulby Newham School. But I think he is entitled to wonder what benefit the trashing of his career and reputation is supposed to achieve, as he looks at the new academy, owned and controlled by car sales mogul, evangelical Christian and friend of Tony Blair, Peter Vardy, now Sir Peter.

King's Academy is controlled by the Emmanuel Schools Foundation, which takes its name from the first school for which Peter Vardy acted as sponsor, Emmanuel College. The Foundation currently controls three schools: Emmanuel College in Gateshead, King's Academy in Middlesbrough and Trinity Academy in Thorne and Moorends, Doncaster. Emmanuel is a city technology college, serving a wide catchment area across Gateshead, Central and West Newcastle and the northern tip of County Durham. King's and Trinity are academies.

Sir Peter was the very first person to come forward and offer money for city academies when David Blunkett announced the scheme in 2000. Without Sir Peter it might never have got beyond the starting line.

Let's look at the three elements of the added value which Sir Peter's sponsorship is supposed to obtain for these schools: his money; his Christianity; and the higher standards which his entrepreneurial flair and Christian ethos are supposed to bring in their wake.

First, the money. Sir Peter put up £2 million for each of his academies, which have of course cost the taxpayer may times that amount. He manages to channel quite a lot of it back into the Vardy and Emmanuel Schools Trust empires. King's Academy paid £111,554 for 'support services such as marketing and recruitment' to his car dealer firm, Reg Vardy plc. It paid £121,514 for 'educational advice' from Emmanuel College, and a £43,107 consultancy fee to Emmanuel's former principal John Burn, now academic adviser to the Emmanuel Schools Foundation. The Billy Graham Evangelistic Association, set up by the world-famous American preacher, was paid £14,039 as reimbursement for time on academy business spent by Sir Peter's brother David.[2] None of this work was put out to tender, which is a legal requirement in state schools. As Gwen Evans, then deputy general secretary of the Association of Teachers and Lecturers, put it: 'Academies were supposed to lever private finance into public education, not lever public money into private pockets.' Nigel McQuoid's explanation on behalf of the Trust, given to me soon after the *TES* revelations, was that the commercial experience, in-house expertise and business contacts of the Vardy organization enabled it to get things done more efficiently and economically than a public sector organization can manage.

Staffing, by the standards of Coulby Newham School, was almost unbelievably generous. Coulby Newham had a senior management team of four and was told it was overstaffed. King's Academy had a senior management team of 14. This is, of course, entirely taxpayer-funded – Sir Peter pays not a penny towards their salaries.

In return for his rather modest investment, Sir Peter's

foundation controls the school totally, with an inbuilt majority on the governing body, where it appoints five out of nine governors.

Second, Christianity – the key to it all. Sir Peter is a creationist. He believes that the Bible is telling the literal truth when it says that the universe was created by God in six days; and that this event occurred in 4004 BC. His foundation also believes that children should be taught that this is the case. 'Schools should teach the creation theory as literally depicted in Genesis,' said Nigel McQuoid when he was head of King's Academy.[3] They now find it convenient to fudge this point, but when I talked to Mr McQuoid in 2004 he said: 'There are scientists who are saying, there are questions about the age of the earth. It's a big issue to say that Darwinism is the only answer. Some new literature is asking some quite interesting scientific questions about it. The children will make up their own minds.'

Mr McQuoid also said: 'The Bible says clearly that homosexual activity is against God's design. I would indicate that to young folk.' Many of us would not wish our children to be taught that, but this does not concern Mr McQuoid, who told a local newspaper: 'I don't have to respect everyone's opinion. I don't respect the opinion of people who believe it's fine to live with a partner. Head teachers are responsible to God and the standards of the Bible. Nothing in the school should contradict the teachings of the Bible.'

'If academies are to succeed', said John Burn, 'they need to be led and staffed by people who are obedient to God's truth as revealed in the scriptures.'[4] So, no teachers who do not hold the approved theological opinions. Burn and Sir Peter form a small committee of two to choose heads for their schools whenever it is necessary, Sir Peter's spokeswoman told me. None of that nonsense about letting parents or teachers have a say.

Mr Burn is one of the founders of the Newcastle-based Christian Institute, set up in 1991 to promote fundamentalist Christian beliefs, and is an outspoken opponent of the ordination of women.

The sort of teacher who went to work at King's Academy may be illustrated by English teacher Peter Fairhurst who defended the practice of preaching hellfire in assembly. 'If assemblies touch on the terrible and eternal consequences of rejecting Jesus Christ they are acting as responsible warnings. We'd all see the necessity of telling children not to accept lifts from strangers or never to dash across busy roads.'[5] Stephen Layfield, head of science at Emmanuel College, gave a long lecture at the college on 21 September 2000 called 'The teaching of science – a biblical perspective'. It reads rather like one of those revivalist sermons, full of Bible-thumping, and it lays down a duty upon teachers to 'do all they can to ensure that pupils, parents and colleagues are reminded frequently that all is not what it seems when popular so-called scientific dogma presents itself before them'. When you find mention of evolution in a textbook, 'point out the fallibility of the statement'. There are separate notes for the teachers of each of the sciences. Apparently, if you are a physics teacher, you are supposed to tell children that the speed of the rotation of the moon proves that God made the earth.

'May it please God', he ends, 'to raise up a new generation of scientists who are duly respectful of their Maker and who, recognizing the limitations of human scientific enquiry, give full weight of respect to the statements of propositional truth of Holy Scripture – being the authoritative word of God.'

Liberal Democrat MP Paul Holmes told the House of Commons: 'Concerns about teaching creationism in science lessons or explaining that God saved us in the Second World

War in history lessons have been aired before. Such people should not be given control of tax-funded state schools.'

The Foundation website, with wonderful doublespeak, calls all this 'an academic and inquisitive approach to spiritual matters including, amongst others, creation and the origin of life on earth'.

But there is also a sinister national agenda here. As long ago as 1995, long before academies became the vehicle for it, it was spelled out in a long booklet from Mr Burn and Mr McQuoid. It is an extraordinary document, and gives us a chilling insight into the long-term agenda of men whom Tony Blair has placed in a powerful position in British education. It says: 'In Britain the Christian churches were active in the field of schooling long before the state took over . . . In retrospect it is a matter of regret that the churches so readily relinquished control of education to the state . . .'

And there you have it. The state must be driven out of education, which should be handed back to the churches. Our function as taxpayers should be confined to providing the money with which people like McQuoid and Burn can make sure we bring up a generation in their own image. What is happening in the north-east is, they hope, a microcosm of what will happen everywhere.

And right now, the law, they think, is on their side: 'It is only by God's sovereignty that current legislation is couched in such advantageous terms in a country where genuine committed Biblical Christian faith is undermined in so many areas.' The very favourable atmosphere for religious indoctrination in schools is, of course, not the work of God but of Tony Blair, though perhaps that is the same thing. Mr Burn and Mr McQuoid are certainly emboldened by the fact that they have the enthusiastic support of Britain's Prime Minister, and Sir Peter's friend, Tony Blair.

Lest there is any doubt that religious indoctrination in schools is what they have in mind, consider this sentence: 'Please do not mistakenly believe that a classroom or school can be neutral: even the absence of a statement can say that no statement is worth the making. As Christ's commission clearly exhorts us, we are to go into all the world, preaching the gospel and making disciples . . . ' I am not sure whether the Emmanuel Schools Foundation's methods are what Christ meant when he said: 'Suffer little children to come unto me.'

After detailing the way in which Christianity should be inculcated in every subject, from literature to geography to pottery, the authors say: 'Christian Truth must play a vital part in all these matters because left to themselves they will be distorted and drained of meaning. Christianity and the Biblical Truth must find a place across the whole curriculum and not just be confined to the act of worship and Religious Education.'[6]

It is a nightmare scenario for British education – that state schools should be controlled by those who are committed to indoctrinating our children with evangelical Christianity. The city academy programme is the best chance they have ever had of making it a reality. 'The Christian ethos of our schools infiltrates all lessons' I was told in 2004 by Sir Peter's spokeswoman Sarah French. 'There will be a Christian assembly every day.'

It is all a million miles from the tolerance and respect of all views and religions that characterized Coulby Newham School. The Royal Society even felt it had to issue a rare protest. Referring specifically to the Emmanuel Schools Foundation, it said: 'Young people are poorly served by deliberate attempts to withhold, distort or misrepresent scientific knowledge and understanding in order to promote particular religious beliefs.' Creationism 'is not consistent with the wealth of evidence for evolution, such as the fossil record. Similarly, a belief that the Earth was formed in 4004 BC is not consistent with the evidence from geology, astronomy and physics that the solar system, including Earth, formed about 4,600 million years ago.'

But, as Tony Blair might have said, never mind the ideology, does it work? No, it doesn't. With the first cohort of GCSE pupils Coulby Newham bequeathed to King's Academy, Coulby Newham anticipated 40 per cent A–C grades at GCSE. The academy set a target of 50 per cent, and achieved 34 per cent, despite expelling ten times as many pupils as the national average. And there were those among the dispossessed at Coulby Newham who suspected that even more were effectively excluded than the published figures suggest. King's Academy should have inherited 285 pupils in Year 11, the GCSE year. It admitted excluding ten of them, which leaves 275. But only 230 sat the examinations. What happened to the other 45 pupils?

We cannot be sure, but the story of young Jack (not his real name) might offer a clue. Jack, aged 15, had been on the verge of exclusion from school more than once in the previous four years, but the teachers always found a way of rescuing him. And then his school was closed, he and the others were moved to the city academy, and Jack's life took a sudden turn for the worse.

The academy required a smart uniform, to be purchased from one particular supplier. His mother Jane (not her real name either) was a single mother with three children, who works part-time. She was eligible for a uniform grant that was tiny. It did not get anywhere near covering the cost, especially as the suppliers did not cater for Jack's size – at 15 he was six feet tall and weighed 17 stone. She bought the uniform, but it hardly got used. Within a week of his school being closed and the pupils being moved to King's Academy, the head, then Mr McQuoid, sent for Jane. She says he advised her to withdraw him, to avoid the stigma of having him expelled, though Mr McQuoid disputes this. She telephoned the local education authority to talk about what Mr McQuoid had said. Officials told her she must wait for the school to expel her son, otherwise no alternative would be found for him.

So the school expelled him, when he was caught smoking a cigarette. Jane pleaded with McQuoid to give her son time to adjust to new, stricter standards. But out he went and, for the rest of Jack's GCSE year, no other local school could be found for him. He was at home for five months. 'He was getting depressed – he suffers from depression anyway. After a time, he just wouldn't come out of his bedroom, not even for his meals,' says Jane. She tried telephoning the head to plead with him, but 'they wouldn't put me through'.

Nor would anyone at the education authority speak to her. 'They'd have been round fast enough if I'd kept him out of school,' says Jane bitterly. 'No one wanted to know.' At last, the following January, the local authority found him a part-time place at a halfway house for excluded pupils. That summer, he sat no GCSEs, so he enrolled himself on a college bricklaying course.

He did well at college. Yet when I got back in touch, in autumn 2006, what King's Academy did to him was still holding him back. Jane told me:

> He's done two years at college, worked hard, passed every-thing, his social skills and business skills courses as well, but he can't get an apprenticeship. He went for an interview and they said, why haven't you got any GCSEs? So he had to tell them why – he'd been thrown out of King's Academy. And they didn't give him an apprenticeship. He's applied to about 30 firms and none of them will take him on.

It's going to be with him for the rest of his life, being expelled, just because he was caught smoking. They let my son down. If he doesn't get an apprenticeship, he can't finish at college, and he's going to look like a school and college dropout, and he'll never get a job.

I wanted to say something comforting, but could find nothing to say. She has made a starkly realistic assessment.

This is just one case, and hard cases make bad law. But if Jack's school had not been closed to make way for a city academy, Jack would probably have finished his schooling, sat some GCSEs, and be in work, or with a job to go to, today.

Of course, the local authority should have found him a place when the academy expelled him. They had a legal obligation to do so, and they failed to meet it. There is no excuse for this, but if they had fulfilled their obligation to him, what then? The effect of allowing academies to exclude pupils, while forcing local authorities to find places for them in their own schools, is to create sink schools. Pupils whom academies do not wish to teach end up in local authority schools, which are then pilloried for getting worse results than academies. Academies are already, as we have seen, vastly better funded than other schools, and they act like leeches, sucking the life out of neighbouring schools.

They also suck the life out of neighbouring sixth-form and further education colleges. In Middlesbrough the local authority was planning for a system of 11–16 schools, with post-16 work to be done in colleges. But local authority planners cannot control what academies will do – only the sponsor can do that. So when academies replace 11–16 schools, they can create a sixth form if they want to. And since they have much more money than either schools or colleges, they are in a position to cream off pupils.

This unsettles colleges. 'No college is going to invest in the future without looking at the numbers', says Julian Gravatt, director of funding and development at the Association of Colleges. Some sixth-form colleges are likely to be forced to close or to merge in order to make room for academies.

St Mary's sixth-form college in Middlesbrough is close to two academies – King's Academy and another not controlled by the Vardy empire, the Unity Academy – which cater for 11–18-year-olds. They both replace schools which catered only for 11–16-year-olds. A third academy is to be created from the existing city technology college, Macmillan College, and it has been given extra capital funding of £10 million, allegedly to ease the transition to city academy status – though it is already substantially richer than local sixth-form colleges.

This creates confusion, said Ofsted in its report on Middlesbrough. 'There is a lack of coherent planning for post-16 provision in Middlesbrough.' This is partly because of 'the recent introduction of a city academy with a sixth form, which is outside the remit of either the local Learning and Skills Council or the LEA'. Plans to increase A-level courses at King's Academy 'have not taken into account the needs of learners in Middlesbrough as a whole'.

Academies are billed as successful replacements for failing schools. But in Middlesbrough, the Unity Academy has already been pronounced a failing school by Ofsted, and, to the irritation of the colleges, has been given an extra £6 million to cope with its unexpected financial shortfall. And, as we have seen, the schools replaced by academies in Middlesbrough were not failing at all.

The third Vardy school, Trinity Academy near Doncaster, was swiftly under fire for the way in which it attempted to impose uniformity on its pupils. The *Guardian*'s Matthew

Taylor reported from a protest meeting in May 2006, a year
after it opened:

> One mother said her daughter had been removed from
> school after being accused of wearing the wrong trousers,
> another that her son had been permanently expelled for
> smoking. A father claimed his son had been sent home for
> walking the wrong way down the corridor, another that his
> 16-year-old daughter was kicked out after getting a kiss from
> her boyfriend at the school gates. And underlying it all was a
> feeling that Trinity, the third state-funded secondary to be
> run by an evangelical Christian and friend of Tony Blair, Sir
> Peter Vardy, was pushing an aggressive religious agenda.
> Cindy Denise, whose two children are both at Trinity,
> claimed pupils were disciplined if they did not carry the Bible
> on certain days and summed up the mood at the meeting,
> describing the school as 'a complete joke'. 'They are kicking
> children out for nothing and won't listen to anyone who
> wants to know what is going on.'
>
> In its first six months 148 children have been suspended,
> leading many parents to claim that it was using excessive dis-
> cipline to weed out children it does not want to teach . . .
>
> Sarah French, a spokeswoman for Sir Peter's Emmanuel
> Schools Foundation, which runs the school, denies the alle-
> gations. 'The idea that we are selecting pupils is a complete
> red herring and really quite offensive. There is no evidence
> whatsoever to support that claim, in fact we give priority to
> children with special educational needs and, although we
> have the right to select 10 per cent of our children by
> aptitude as an academy, we don't because we aim to help each
> child achieve its potential . . .

Cindy Denise told Matthew Taylor: 'It's not what I want my kids to be doing in school, but I don't have a choice because this is the only school round here and they won't listen to us.'[7]

And it's the idea that children are forced to go to some of Vardy's schools, for lack of an alternative, which led to a great defeat for Sir Peter – a local uprising which shows that, even with the power of the state behind them, academies can sometimes be stopped by people power.

It happened near Doncaster. In two mining villages, the Conisbrough and Denaby Parents' Action Group decided to fight the proposal to close their local secondary school, Northcliffe. 'At the end of April 2004 we became worried that a religious sect was to take over our children's education and school. All manner of gossip was spreading through the village, some knew more than others. Officially we were told very little. Parents are able to make informed and reasonable decisions about the future and education of their children, but can only do so if given accurate unbiased information', says its website.[8]

The council allowed a one-month 'consultation' which parents say was a sham.

> To most people the idea of 'consultation' means listening to both views and then deciding or voting on the idea. This is not what consultation means to the LEA and the Vardy group. To them it means presentation. The 'consultation' meetings that have been scheduled are rushed, brief and the agenda firmly fixed in favour of pushing through an academy as quickly as possible.

By June 2003, consultation was done and dusted, so far as the council and the Vardy people were concerned. Local people, according to a council spokesman, had 'been given ample opportunity to voice any concerns'. But there was a problem here which did not apply so much in urban areas. Northcliffe was the only available choice for many local parents. If it fell into the hands of religious fundamentalists, they would not have the chance of sending their children somewhere else. They really were being told: if you want your children educated at all, Bible-thumping will be part of the package.

By the start of July, the Conisbrough and Denaby Parents' Action Group had gathered close to 1,000 signatures on an anti-Vardy petition. The council hedged, held more consultation meetings at which Vardy's people tried to fudge the religion issue, but on Wednesday 13 October, Doncaster's mayor bowed to public pressure and announced that Northcliffe Comprehensive would remain open, and that the Vardy plan was binned.

Sir Peter Vardy, clearly irritated, offered a remarkably un-Christian reflection. 'Far from celebrating, [the Parents' Action Group] should be reflecting on the opportunity they have denied their children for an education of the very highest standard in state-of-the-art facilities.' He grudged them their victory, and thought that the parents were being triumphalist. But he was wrong. The parents were not at all triumphalist. Their website simply says: 'Ours is not a victory but a second chance for Northcliffe and for state education in our area.'

There would, of course, have been nothing to stop Sir Peter from giving his money anyway, and the Government from providing public money anyway, to establish the school the parents wanted rather than the school Sir Peter wanted. But the people of Conisbrough and Denaby have defied Government ideology. Their children will not get any of Sir Peter's millions, nor any of the state money that only comes with Sir Peter's blessing. They will do the best they can for their children without it. Good luck to them.

Nigel McQuoid did not want to be interviewed for this book. He was kind enough, however, to telephone and tell me so himself, a courtesy one does not get from everyone, and we had an off-the-record general conversation. I don't think I am betraying any confidences if I say that he is upset and puzzled at the way I and others write about the Vardy schools. He feels that he and Sir Peter have been unjustly pilloried, when all they want to do is to provide a better education for the poorest children. I have little doubt that Mr McQuoid is perfectly sincere, and believes he is doing good.

I get the impression that Sir Peter himself is surprised and hurt at the world's ingratitude. Just a couple of years ago his spokeswoman Sarah French was telling me about his plans to have six academies and be responsible for the education of 10,000 young people; now he does not seem to want to expand beyond his current three.

However odd Sir Peter Vardy is, his close friend Mr Robert Edmiston, sponsor of the academy in Solihull, is odder. He too made a fortune from the car business – in his case by importing Japanese cars – and used his millions to set up Christian Vision (CV) whose website says it is 'committed to bringing people into a relationship with Jesus and has developed a number of global strategies to achieve this, including "Touch a Billion" and "Impact a Nation"'. It exists 'to introduce people to Jesus and encourage those who acknowledge Him to accept Him as the Son of God and become His true followers'.

He has put more than £60 million into Christian Vision, which broadcasts by satellite from Birmingham to developing countries, offering music and Bible-thumping pastors.

The mindset of a man who thinks that, beset as the developing world is by famine and war, what it really needs is Bible-thumping on the Internet, is one I find hard to understand. Still, it's his money, and he has a right to spend it how he likes.

What he does not have a right to is control over state education and the public resources that go with it. But that is what the Government has given him. His school too will teach creationism, and his defence for this is far more bizarre than anything Sir Peter Vardy has come up with. 'If you tell people they are descended from monkeys how can you expect them to behave like anything other than monkeys?' he says.[9]

Edmiston sponsored and controls Grace Academy in Solihull. It is named as a tribute to Mr Edmiston's faith – it comes from the American evangelical movement, and there are many schools called Grace in the USA. He is also to sponsor a new academy to replace Woodway Park school in Coventry, which will probably also be called Grace.

He is putting in £2 million of the £31 million that the lavish building he has had designed will cost. Of course, all the initial costs – consultants' fees, surveys, investigation on site – were paid for by the DfES. All the many meetings consultants and the rest need to have were held in Coleshill Manor, owned by Mr Edmiston, and the DfES was charged just like a commercial client for hiring the room and having tea and biscuits laid on. It is, as it happens, the same building which Mr Edmiston used to assist the Conservative Party, but unlike the taxpayer, the Conservative Party was not required to pay for its use.

Coleshill Manor is set in 200 acres of parkland and protected by 24-hour security, and it is home to Constituency Campaigning Services, a strategy centre charged with targeting 164 marginal seats on behalf of the Conservative Party.

Will Woodward described it in the *Guardian*:

It is both a campaign centre and a call centre. Over two floors it employed up to 50 people at the height of the last election. Since David Cameron became Conservative leader, work at the centre has been stepped up significantly. More staff are being recruited to offer 24-hour advice to all constituencies, designing and printing their literature, advising on how to recruit new members, and conducting market research on public opinion on key issues.

Edmiston refunds to Conservative Campaign Services the money they spend on hiring the building – £100,000 by October 2006. Police are investigating the fact that this does not appear as a gift on the Conservative Party's returns (more on this in Chapter 3). But Mr Edmiston does not offer the same generosity to the taxpayer-funded education service to which he is supposed to be committed. The DfES must pay for every room in which Mr Edmiston calls a meeting to discuss academy business.

The Grace Academy is a new school built on the site of Whitemore School near Solihull – a deprived area to which people were decamped in the 1960s when the Bullring was built. Whitemore, of course, was not a failing school, or in special measures. The Grace Academy's specialism, as if you hadn't guessed, will be business and enterprise, and the staff are expected to uphold Christian principles.

*   *   *

Christian sponsors fall into four categories.

There are the militants – the evangelicals and creationists. These are Vardy with his three academies, and Edmiston with one and another on the way.

There are the Roman Catholics, with three academies, in Greenwich, Lewisham and Liverpool; and the Church of England, with five, in Merton, Haringey, Bradford, Leeds and Leicester.

And there are the Anglican trusts. These are led by the biggest academy sponsor of all, the United Learning Trust, a subsidiary of the United Church Schools Trust, which runs eight academies, in Manchester, Salford, Lambeth, Paddington, Northampton, Barnsley and Sheffield (where it will have two academies) and plans to sponsor no fewer than 20. The other player, Oasis, a Christian trust, will control an academy in Enfield to open in September 2007, and four more later in Grimsby, Immingham, Bristol and Salford. Oasis was founded by Steve Chalke, another evangelical Christian.

Mr Chalke has caused a great ideological split in the evangelical movement, because Mr Chalke's book *The Lost Message of Jesus* questioned the idea that God punished his son by sending him to the cross – otherwise known, apparently, as 'penal substitution'.

Oasis academies will be 'rooted in Christian-based core values, which it is hoped will permeate every aspect of its life'. But Oasis is firmly against giving any favoured treatment to Christians, and Mr Chalke condemns those Christian organizations, like the Roman Catholics, which resist pressure to take pupils who are not of the faith in their state schools. 'You can either have a school only for Christians or a Christian school. You can't have both', he says. 'A Christ-centred school will serve the whole community.' And he is not a creationist. In fact, his reading of Genesis directly contradicts Sir Peter Vardy's. He thinks the idea that God made the world in six days is only meant as a parable. After all, he says, if God did not make the sun and the moon until the third day, how were the days counted until then, since there was no sun to rise?

In 2000 Mr Chalke founded xalt.co.uk whose home page, when I looked, began with the startling claim that the BBC is institutionally biased against Christianity. It consists mostly of simple religious homilies, quotations from the Bible, and advertisements for religious books. It offers 'Exalt-txt – a unique service which delivers a verse of the Bible direct to your mobile/cell phone daily. Ideal as a gift to encourage a friend/relative.'

Apart from the academies they directly control, the Church of England has a presence among the sponsors of several other academies. Thus, for example, in the Isle of Sheppey, though it is putting in no money, its name is among the sponsors so that it can ensure, as diocesan education officer Rupert Bristow put it to me, that 'Christian values should underpin the academy'.

'Christian values' is the most mischievous phrase in the language, for it refers to values which are common to those of all religions and none – truthfulness, honesty, care for others, that sort of thing. For Christians to call them 'Christian values' is to colonize them, and deny that non-Christians can share them.

Between them, they are massively increasing the power of Christianity over state education through the city academy programme. But does this do any real harm? That depends partly on what the Christian sponsors want to do with their power. And here the news is bad. They have their own agenda.

Creationists want to turn the clock back to the days when the churches controlled education. We have already seen how the creationists view it: 'In retrospect it is a matter of regret that the churches so readily relinquished control of education to the state.' The city academy programme can be the lever which brings education back under the control of the churches.

This thinking is strong in the Roman Catholic Church as well. I had occasion to speak recently on another story to Michael McGrath, education officer for the Roman Catholic

Church in Scotland. 'Catholic schools in Scotland were transferred in 1918 to the state and the church was then guaranteed
certain rights', he told me.

The matter on which I contacted Mr McGrath was a story
about a teacher in a Roman Catholic state school who had been
denied an interview for promotion because he was an atheist,
and took his case to an employment tribunal. He won, but only
on a technicality, and it was a double-edged victory. Mr
McGrath gave me his take on the judgement.

'All teachers in state Catholic schools in Scotland require the
approval of the Catholic church in terms of religious belief and
character. The judgement reaffirmed that this still applies, and
to any teaching post. We do approve non-Catholic teachers for
certain posts – we make a judgement about religious beliefs and
character.' On Mr McGrath's interpretation, Roman Catholic
schools can refuse to employ a teacher on grounds of faith, or
on grounds of morality – for example, they can refuse to employ
a teacher on the grounds that the teacher is divorced.

They can count on support from their old enemies the evangelicals. 'If academies are to succeed,' says John Burn of the
Emmanuel Schools Foundation, 'they need to be led and staffed
by people who are obedient to God's truth as revealed in the
scriptures.' So, no teachers who do not hold the approved theological opinions.

Meanwhile the Catholic Education Service said in 2006 that
it will 'robustly oppose' Education Secretary Alan Johnson's
proposal for 25 per cent of children at faith schools to be of a
non-faith or different faith background. In its academies the
Roman Catholic Church has argued to be allowed to discrimi-
nate in favour of Roman Catholics when it comes to admissions.

The Roman Catholics expect to have it both ways: to have the
state pay for schools in which only Catholic children are allowed

to learn and only teachers approved by the church are allowed to
teach. But this is the way with faith groups. The *Jewish Chronicle*
on 20 October 2006 reported 'outrage' at Mr Johnson's proposal.
Joshua Rowe, chair of governors at Manchester King David High
school, called it 'an absolute tragedy' adding: '[Jewish schools] are
the best schools in the country and you cannot run them if a
quarter of your intake is not of the faith.' Why on earth not?

Mr Johnson swiftly backtracked. The shadow of what the late
Ted Wragg used to call Tony Zoffis still hangs heavy over the
DfES, and it took less than a week to kick Mr Johnson into
unconditional surrender to the religious lobby.

Back in 2002, the Church of England made its motives for
being in the education business startlingly clear in a document
calling for more state-funded faith schools. It was alarmingly
frank about what they were to be used for. The Church, it said,
is involved in education to 'nourish those of faith, encourage
those of other faiths, challenge those who have no faith'. Why
only 'challenge' those who have no faith?

The document explained that church schools 'offer opportunities to pupils and their families to explore the truths of the
Christian faith'. You're not supposed, in these schools, to
question Christianity; you're supposed to 'explore' its 'truths'.
The Church of England is in the education business to get 'em
young, because that, as the Jesuits discovered centuries ago, is
the best chance you have of keeping them.

The Church wants its schools to give preference to parents
with Christian backgrounds, to employ more Christian
teachers, and to make sure Christian teachers get preference
when it comes to promotion. Heads in particular must be committed Christians. So the more Church of England schools we
have, the more teachers will depend for their career prospects on
holding the correct religious beliefs.

They should, says the document, reserve some places 'for children of other faiths, and perhaps even of no faith'. I like 'perhaps even'. My children might stand a chance, if we could find a school generous enough to overlook their parents' deplorable paganism. Once there, non-Christian children 'will experience what it is like to live in a community that celebrates the Christian faith'. They will also be forced to say Christian prayers.

Even the architect of city technology colleges believes this is a dangerous development. Kenneth Baker, Education Secretary from 1986 to 1989 and now Lord Baker, scorned to rescue his doomed enterprise with this stratagem, rejecting proposals from Christian, Muslim and Jewish organizations to found schools. 'I regret that the government has adopted its (faith schools) policy because I think that the new faith schools have become very exclusive', he said in 1986.[10]

At a time when – via the city academies programme – Christian churches are gaining control of more schools than they have ever controlled before, it looks as though more young adults, and more teachers, will have the ministrations of the Church forced upon them.

Notes

1. *Newcastle Journal.*
2. NUT Briefing, *Academies: Looking Beyond the Spin*, 2006.
3. *Guardian*, 15 January 2005.
4. Lecture reprinted by the Christian Institute, 12 October 2000.
5. *Times Educational Supplement*, 30 May 2004.
6. *Christianity and the School Curriculum*, Christian Institute, 1995.
7. Matthew Taylor, *Guardian*, 30 May 2006.
8. http://www.cadpag.pwp.blueyonder.co.uk/index.html
9. Quoted by Liberal Democrat MP Paul Holmes in the House of Commons.
10. *Times Educational Supplement*, 17 February 2006.

6

A Learning Curve in West London

It must have seemed a good idea to take three schools on the same site – a secondary, a primary, and a school for children with special needs – and bring them together into one new state-of-the-art building, knocking down the three existing buildings. And it might have been a good idea, if it had been done sensitively by people who understood state education. As it is, it's been a catalogue of expensive disasters smothered with a veneer of meaningless management jargon.

The new building was designed by Sir Norman Foster, the man responsible for the Gherkin, a famous and highly unusual London office block, and the Millennium Bridge, but without school building experience. He created one long curved corridor as a centrepiece, and called it, with that flair for a soundbite which often does duty for meaning, a 'learning curve'. It is designed so that you cannot see the whole length of it from the inside, and is a quarter of a mile long. 'He gave us an office block that looked like an aircraft hangar', said one teacher.

Foster was taken on by the academy's sponsor, Alec Reed, of Reed Employment, who carefully protected his position right from the start, back in 2001, promising to pay one-fifth of the set-up costs – but only to a maximum of £2 million. Reed was lavish with our money, and the building cost a fabulous £37 million. Reed's contribution is therefore just over one-twentieth of the capital cost, and none of the running costs at all. For this he gains ownership and control of the academy in perpetuity, and he can – and does – spend as much taxpayers' money as he likes.

Some of this money goes into Reed's own enterprises. The academy paid £140,030 to Reed Charity, chaired by Mr Reed; £37,683 to Reed Learning; and £3,251 to Reed Training. None of this work was put out to tender, which is a legal requirement in state schools.

So what does Reed bring to the table in return for all this taxpayers' largesse? Here's how the DfES website describes his contribution:

> Alec Reed brings his entrepreneurial skills and expertise in leadership, innovation and enterprise from the Academy of Enterprise and his successful recruitment business to the West London Academy. His expertise means that the pupils are more responsible and more entrepreneurial and that enterprise underpins much of the curriculum . . .

It's not at all clear how his expertise can make pupils any of these things. Perhaps they are supposed to absorb responsibility and entrepreneurship from the mere aura of Reed, through their pores. Or perhaps the secret lies in the idea that 'Each year group has its own cluster of classrooms, arranged around a recreation area or "enterprise zone".' It is unclear what makes this area an 'enterprise zone'. Does calling it an enterprise zone turn all the pupils into little entrepreneurs?

His first head teacher, Alastair Falk, thinks there was some added value from Reed's involvement. Reed created a human resources function and an accounting function which most schools do not have, and which an enterprise of that size should have, says Falk.

Falk joined in October 2002 and was the highest paid head teacher in the country. Previously head of King Solomon High School in Redbridge, he was appointed on a salary and benefits package reportedly worth £120,000. (Falk says it was less, but will not say how much less, though he was paid from public funds.) At any rate, he beat the state system's highest paid head, Michael Murphy, a so-called 'super-head' hired two years previously for £96,000 to turn round Crown Woods school in south-east London. Most state school heads were then getting under £50,000, and even private school heads seldom earned more than £80,000.

Falk, from all accounts, is a nice man who likes children. I found him a thoughtful and committed educationalist, and not at all the sort of Thatcherite ideologue whom you often find in city academies. But anyone with experience of state education could have told Reed, had he been in the mood to listen to such people, that Falk's experience of successfully running King Solomon School, a faith school which describes itself as 'serving the Jewish communities of Redbridge and surrounding areas', was no preparation for running a school with a mixed and often difficult intake.

He accepts that the academy was not replacing a failing school, but 'a school which was suffering from lack of investment'. This is true. It is also true that it was starved of state funding, and therefore forced to give place to Mr Reed's academy.

The school opened in September 2003, in the existing building because the new one was still being built. And when Ofsted came to visit, in July 2005, it found a mess. Exam results 'were well below the national figures and those of schools in similar socio-economic circumstances' – in many subjects worse than those in the secondary school which the academy replaced.

Most of the teachers were new, appointed by the academy rather than inherited from the predecessor school, yet teaching was 'significantly weaker than the national profile' (though some of it was excellent). Attendance and punctuality were poor. The curriculum lacked 'breadth and balance' with no coherent personal and social education, and no modern foreign languages. The much-vaunted specialism in enterprise was 'not evident in its provision'. The governors, even though they had got rid of those meddlesome parent and staff representatives, could not manage to create systems which would allow them to chart the academy's progress.

Many teachers had low expectations and could not keep order, though the academy boasted an innovative system of sanctions and rewards for behaviour, which Ofsted found were applied inconsistently and had not been discussed with staff. And this was despite a very high rate of exclusions. 265 pupils had been excluded, and a further 20 permanently excluded, out of just 746 pupils. The academy failed to analyse information about exclusions rigorously.

And what of the expensive head? He had a vision and communicated it, but there were 'crucial areas' of his 'leadership and management that are unsatisfactory' and he was not communicating with his staff effectively.

'Inconsistency pervades the work of the academy', wrote the lead inspector, Boyd Gunnell. 'The visit has raised serious concerns about the standard of education provided by the academy and I am recommending an early return visit.'

Nick Grant, the local NUT secretary, says: 'For any other comparable school this would be a scandalous report. High exclusion rates normally means double figures, not treble. The head would have been sacked at once and the school put under the direct control of the DfES.'

These problems were hardly surprising, given the state of the teaching staff. The experienced and mostly competent staff from the predecessor schools had been scattered to the four winds. Some had been offered generous settlements to go quietly. These included the activists in teacher trade unions. Perhaps this is coincidental, but the academy has still not agreed to negotiate with trade unions, despite numerous approaches.

But many staff simply left, disliking the way things were going, and found jobs in local authority schools. Nick Grant says: 'Initially the West London Academy solved this by paying way over the odds to attract young teachers, putting many of them on the Senior Management Scale. Inflated salaries are no longer offered to staff, but the turnover remains phenomenal. They have used the revolving door of agency staff to fill the gaps.'

Within weeks of the Ofsted report we learned that the academy's GCSE results were actually worse than those in the predecessor school. Falk insists that he was not fired, but Reed gave him a job running the Academy for Enterprise, an organization Reed had set up to 'inject a spirit of enterprise throughout the entire British way of life'. His replacement was the much more ferocious Hilary Macaulay, previously vice-principal at the ADT city technology college in Wandsworth.

Ms Macaulay has acquired a reputation for ruthlessness and intolerance of criticism. One former teacher, for whom it was her first job, told me:

I gave my notice to her, and said I was going to work for an ordinary state school. She asked me what I thought of the academy, didn't I think it was wonderful, what an opportunity I was missing to leave it all and go to just an ordinary school. I said there was no discipline in the academy, I'd had children swearing at me and there wasn't enough support, and I'd been to the ordinary school and the children there were wonderful by comparison. I said staff morale was low, and she said, well, some people aren't suited to this opportunity and they will leave. I criticized the system where we had to send emails to her when a child behaved well and she monitored the time the emails had been sent.

Ms Macaulay declined to speak to me. Her office said she is 'not very keen on handing out information'. One piece of information she does not hand out is the 2006 examination results. Nick Grant believes there is a good reason to keep them under wraps. Early in 2006, Ofsted came back for the return visit Mr Gunnell had promised. This time Mr Gunnell's summary was: 'The academy has made good progress since July 2005. Nevertheless, this visit has raised some concerns about the standard of education provided and the academy's performance will be monitored.' Achievement and standards were 'inadequate'.

Ms Macaulay was furious about the press coverage and sent all her staff a long, semi-literate tirade by email.

Other schools and national bodies who had previously enjoyed the fact that some could languish at the bottom of a discriminatory pile seem quick to apportion negativity on the Academy movement and show total ignorance over such issues as . . . who actually runs the school (believe it or not I have had it frequently misquoted by those outside the academies movement that the sponsor does); that we get more money than other schools (our funding is directly in line with other local authority schools) . . .

Of course, the sponsor does run academies, and the huge capital sum which the Government gives to academies is not available to any other sort of school. Whether Ms Macaulay does not know that, or was trying to mislead her staff, it is impossible to be sure. 'I can't imagine what it must be like to make a deliberate choice to reflect the negative such as some journalists or individuals do', she wrote.

But perhaps the most serious casualty of this expensive and unsuccessful experiment was the school for children with special needs, John Chilton School. At first John Chilton's governors wanted to be part of a project which they thought would give their children access to better facilities, but they were turned down. Governors and staff were not too upset about this, for they already had a school they were justly proud of. Their existing 24-year-old building was all on one level – important because many of their children have disabilities which prevent them climbing stairs – and the local authority had recently spent money on it, providing new windows, double glazing, electric doors and other facilities. The school had a friendly, almost family atmosphere. No one has ever suggested that John Chilton was anything other than a first-class, well-run special needs school.

The new academy was designed to house the secondary school and the primary only. Then, at the last moment, the decision was taken to bring John Chilton into the new building – not as part of the new academy, but as a separate school, in the middle of the building, between the area allocated to the secondary school and that allocated to the primary school. Why the change of mind? Some of John Chilton's teachers bearded Reed on one of his visits to the site. He told them it would look bad in the media if the special needs school was excluded.

Reed did not bring them in for free, however. The local authority had to give his academy an extra £5 million to build

John Chilton into the building, and will have to pay rent for ever to Reed's academy for housing John Chilton. It will even have to pay rent for the parking spaces used by John Chilton's teachers and its two minibuses. These minibuses proved one of the least important, but most niggling, of the problems. They had been given to John Chilton by the Variety Club of Great Britain, which insisted that they be kept in a garage, since otherwise they risked being vandalized. The garages were to be pulled down, since they did not fit in with Reed's and Sir Norman Foster's vision of the site. The architects insisted that any new garages had to have a special finish which would have brought the cost of building them up to £80,000, for otherwise they felt it would spoil the look of their splendid building. No one was prepared to find £80,000. So, no garages.

More important, John Chilton's new home was to be on two floors, instead of one; there were no ramps on the stairs; and there is only one lift, which can only be used by a pupil when accompanied by a teacher. 'You're taking away our pupils' independence', one of the teachers who bearded Reed said. 'What independence?' asked the sponsor. The corridor – sorry, 'learning curve' – runs the length of the building, so pupils and teachers use it as a short cut between the secondary and primary school. John Chilton's entrance is an afterthought at the back of the building, originally intended as a fire door.

Teachers arrived in September 2005 a week before the children, to find they were working in a building site. Building workers were all wearing hard hats. This information appeared in a national newspaper, and John Chilton's head Simon Rosenberg gave his staff a dressing down about leaking information. Teachers and children from John Chilton watched through their windows as their old school was knocked down. John Chilton, I'm told, is now a shadow of its former self.

7

Islington Feels the Wrath of Downing Street

Islington – once home to Tony Blair, still home to Lord Adonis – was of special interest to the Government. But perhaps we would not have predicted the level of interest. The amount of direct interference in Islington's affairs, often coming right from the top in Downing Street, has been extraordinary.

Islington Green School has had a rocky ride for more than a decade, at least with the press. Tony Blair, when he was opposition leader, lived nearby, and there was a political row when he decided instead to send his own sons to the other side of London, to the opted-out London Oratory which selected its pupils by interviewing the boy together with both his parents. Blair's close friend and education guru Andrew Adonis, now Lord Adonis, still lives nearby, and the school, or whatever replaces it, could easily be the local secondary school for his children.

In 1997, Ofsted chief Chris Woodhead placed the school on 'special measures', stating that it had failed its inspection, against the unanimous advice of his own inspectors, who visited the school and said it had passed. Mr Woodhead's role was not discovered until January 2005, when a teacher at the school and its NUT representative, Ken Muller, used the Freedom of Information Act to prove it.

The killer memo was from one of the inspectors, Barry Jones, to Chris Woodhead. He says the team 'were of the unanimous view that the school was not failing', even though they already knew that they were under pressure to say that it was. 'A few days later we read in the papers that the school had been put into special measures.' He made sure his superiors knew how unhappy he was, and was promised an explanation, but never received one. 'Even after this passage of time I am still uneasy about the final judgement and the lack of feedback to the team members', he wrote.

What on earth was going on? Here are a few facts, and a healthy dollop of speculation. Islington Green School has had enemies in high places ever since it embarrassed the Blairs by being the local school to which they did not wish to send their children. It would be politically convenient for them if it were a failing school; it would make their decision look less like mere snobbery. In 1997, Blair's first year in power, Blair and Woodhead were very close, and Blair saved Woodhead's job by preventing Education Secretary David Blunkett from firing him.

The idea that Woodhead might have failed the school as a political favour to the Prime Minister who saved his job seems so appallingly cynical that one recoils from it. It may be that Mr Woodhead has a perfectly good explanation for his actions, although none has been forthcoming.

The Ofsted judgement looked for a while as though it might be self-fulfilling, as such judgements often are. It certainly caused a crisis of confidence at the school. But the school recovered. It is a good school, and getting steadily better, the highest achieving mixed school in Islington in the value added tables. It is doing a lot better than most academies. Ken Muller asked Dr Terry Wrigley, an Edinburgh University education lecturer and editor of the journal *School Improvement*, to examine its effectiveness and compare it with existing academies. Wrigley did so and wrote to Muller:

When I examined data published for Islington Green School, this revealed a very different pattern [from academies]: improvement on the second measure, i.e. including English and Maths, was high, from 19 to 24 between 2002 and 2005 – an improvement nearly ten times as great as the existing academies.

I was also able to examine other aspects of attainment at Islington Green, and in particular the situation of lower attaining pupils. Here you show a dramatic improvement. I found data going back to 2001, when only 72 per cent of pupils gained five A*–Gs. In 2005 it was 91 per cent. In fact, none of the Academies can match this: in 2005 they range from 66 per cent to 90 per cent, and half of them are below 80 per cent.

Looking at pupils leaving Islington Green without a single GCSE, this has shrunk from 13 per cent in 2001 to 2 per cent in 2005. Obviously it is difficult to do much better, but over half of the academies do worse (up to 10 per cent leaving without a single GCSE) . . .

Islington Green has a good local reputation and fast improving examination results.

At the beginning of 2004 Blair's former chief speech-writer, Peter Hyman, arrived at the school in the unusual capacity of a teaching assistant on the senior management team with special responsibility for public relations. One of the first tasks assigned to him by the head teacher was to facilitate the creation of a twin-site 3–19 academy to replace Islington Green School and one of its feeder schools, Moreland Primary. Hyman cheerfully told other staff that he often met Blair socially and they discussed the affairs of the school. In 2004 he obtained the services of Alastair Campbell to speak at the school.

The forces against Islington Green School were assembling. Education researcher Dr Richard Hatcher has listed them to show how formidable an enemy they made:

> The Academies Division of the DfES, providing political and logistical support to the local projects; the London Diocesan Board of the Church of England; 3Es, a private project management company employed by the Diocesan Board to front the Church bid; ARK [Absolute Return for Kids], the charitable trust run by bankers and investors; Cambridge Education, the private company running the outsourced Islington LEA; school managers (head teachers and school governing bodies).
>
> On the other side of the Islington argument were parents, teachers and local residents, with no powerful institutional backing. They were dependent on voluntary commitment, mostly given in their own time and on social resources, in the form of networking, of the ad hoc campaigning bodies they set up, and of the organizational support of school union groups and the local association structures of the NUT.

There was an extraordinary row over who was to sponsor the new academy, which tells us a great deal about how the programme is run – and who really runs it.

Islington missed out on the first round of Building Schools for the Future money, mainly because it had no plans for an academy. Its ruling Liberal Democrat councillors, though they oppose academies, realized that unless they agreed to go down the academy route, they would be forced to watch Islington's schools crumble and decay from lack of money. The present council leader, James Kempton, has told friends that he does not want academies, but that if he does not have them, he will be denied any money to spend on Islington's schools. So the council negotiated a deal with the City of London Corporation for the latter to sponsor an academy. The Corporation was not exactly private sector, but it was deeply conservative and run by businessmen, so no doubt Islington councillors thought that would be enough to satisfy the Prime Minister.

But someone in Downing Street had a better idea, and at the start of 2005 Islington was told that it would only get approval – and the cash that goes with it – if it changed sponsors. The sponsor Downing Street wanted was ARK, a charity run by a group of millionaire merchant bankers and hedge fund speculators.

ARK is close to the Prime Minister. When Blair's chief of staff, Sally Morgan, left Downing Street, she went to work for ARK. Its website offers lavish thanks to Lord Levy, the Prime Minister's tennis partner and chief fundraiser (whose role was discussed in Chapter 3), for helping it auction a game of tennis with Mr Blair at its charity dinner.

Ken Muller says:

ARK's website claims they have a wealth of experience. What they do have is an experience of wealth. First on the list of ARK corporate sponsors is Aspect Capital whose Aspect Funds are 'organized as exempted companies incorporated with limited liability in the Cayman Islands' and 'not overseen by the Caymans Island government or any other regulator'. One of ARK's directors, Jennifer Moses, and her husband Ron Beller, were famously robbed of £2 million by their secretary Joyti DeLaurey – the amount a private sponsor is meant to pay in return for being given control of a £30 million academy – in 2004 without noticing it was missing.

So Islington councillors were forced to change tack if they wanted money for Islington schools. They talked to ARK. The then council leader, Liberal Democrat Steve Hitchins, said: 'This confusion in government is very disappointing, and it is hard to construct real partnerships on these shifting sands. However, now it is settled, we are very happy to be working with ARK.'[1]

In June, demonstrators in fat cat suits lobbied ARK's head-quarters, and the London *Evening Standard* reported that following 'a protest outside the charity's Westminster offices last week by parents and teachers against "fat cats" taking over state schools . . . Tony Blair's plan for city academies was dealt a major blow today after a millionaire backer pulled out of a London project'. ARK had pulled out. It had nothing to do with the protest, they said. The reason given was that ARK had decided that an all-through school would not work. But it took them a long time to reach this conclusion, and it seems likely that ARK's directors did not like working in the eye of high-profile political controversy.

The head teacher at Islington Green, Trevor Averre-Beason, who had been strongly in favour of the academy proposal, called his staff together and told them it would still go ahead somehow. Most of his staff opposed the academy, but he assured them they would not be able to stop it.

On the other hand, at the primary school, Moreland, governors met and further complicated the matter by pulling out of the academy proposal entirely. The all-through academy was dead. If ARK had only been concerned about that aspect, this was the time for them to return. But they did not.

The council went back to their old sponsors, the Corporation of London, to see if they could kiss and make up. They could. The Corporation offered £1 million, and City University came in with another £1 million. This time it was to be an 11–19 school, replacing Islington Green School. Moreland was reprieved.

It is worth pointing out that both the Corporation and the University are public institutions run on public money. There is not a penny of private sector cash being leveraged into state education here.

City University's reason, it said, was that it is a local university situated not far from the school, and wants to cement links with secondary schools. Of course, you can cement links with secondary schools without controlling them. Universities are crying poverty and demanding to be allowed to raise students' tuition fees in order to make ends meet. City's students may have something to say about the spending of £1 million of their money on the Government's academy programme.

The new wheeze was advertised in a glossy booklet called, inevitably, *Aiming Higher: City of London Academy Islington*. Protesters have already said they 'consider it unreasonable to make a decision on these matters without knowing what is to be in the funding agreement which will determine such crucial matters as admissions, exclusions and SEN provision'.

The Expression of Interest states that the academy will 'specialize in Business and Enterprise linked to financial Services' (it had better not specialize in English, if its sponsors use initial capitals in this illiterate way). In the *Aiming Higher* booklet it has been changed to 'Education for the World of Work' which will 'prepare our students to be enterprising and successful in business and the professions; develop the skills necessary for the full range of career and work opportunities associated with the City of London'.

Local parent Julie Hunt wrote to the *Islington Tribune* in May

2006: 'My children will be of working age soon enough and until that time I believe they should have the right to a rounded education, as should all children.'

It seems likely that the academy will actually decrease the amount of space given to the school. The draft planning guidance says: 'Residential units may also be accommodated on the site if this provision does not adversely affect the school.'

Lord Adonis is the minister who is supposed to make the decision about whether to agree to an 'expression of interest' from the Corporation, but protestors have pointed out that his two children, who attend an Islington primary school, stand to benefit if the £30 million project goes ahead. The task of saying yes had to be performed by one of his colleagues.

Events over the summer of 2006 have given protestors some hope that the juggernaut can still be halted. In July the council's so-called Overview Committee, after noisy and well-supported lobbying, split evenly on the academy proposal, 4–4, and it went through on the chair's casting vote. The closure notice was to have been issued on 4 September, but the NUT gave notice that it will seek judicial review of the decision. Almost all the teachers oppose the academy proposal.

But it looks as though councillors and ministers are determined not to give Islington Green School any chance to maintain the momentum of its success. Half the senior management team departed in summer 2006. And then, in the second week of the autumn term, the head teacher, Trevor Averre-Beason, called all his staff together for an important announcement.

Averre-Beason had supported the academy idea through thick and thin. Despite this, his staff liked him, and thought him a good head – which he must have been, because the school under a poor head could not have maintained Islington Green's steady improvement. He probably hoped to lead the new academy.

At the meeting, staff could see that he was deeply upset. He told them he was leaving the job, and would be going at half-term. This is an extraordinary way to do things. A head teacher never leaves halfway through the term. It is well understood in teaching that you serve out the term, both to ensure continuity and to give the school time to find a new head.

But why did Averre-Beason go? He was happy and successful in the job. He had turned the school round after it was sent into a downward spiral when Chris Woodhead labelled it a failing school. Just seven months previously, Roy Hattersley was writing of him in the *Guardian*:

> Two dramatic indicators of success confirm Averre-Beeson's achievement. Four years ago, Islington Green advertised for an assistant head. There were three candidates. Two of them were unsuitable. This year the school advertised again, and there were 46 applicants . . . He provides the second example of success. Confidence has been restored. Last July, when the school learned of the London suicide bombings, most pupils wanted to stay on site. That is where they felt safe . . . Asked if, ten years ago, he would have sent his children to Islington Green, he chooses, with proper professional discretion, to answer a different question. 'I would certainly send them here now.'

What on earth would make such a head walk out of the job suddenly, without warning, halfway through the term? I'm told, on good authority, that he didn't jump – he was pushed; and that authority for pushing him came from outside Islington. In Islington these days they say 'Downing Street' in a meaningful way. There were rumours that he was losing his initial enthusiasm for the academy project. He had also given staff a personal assurance that he would not allow pay and conditions to become worse. They accepted his sincerity, but pointed out that he might leave the school.

An even harder body blow came when Cambridge Education Associates – the private education consultancy which the Government appointed some years ago to take control of Islington education – told the school that its £260,000 deficit, which was to be paid off over several years, must now be paid off in two years. They insisted on payment before the school closed and the academy opened.

This was a dreadful financial blow in a school whose finances were already stretched, and about 14 teachers were made redundant so that the money could be paid. Class sizes have risen sharply. A good school in a poor area is being vandalized before the academy is even agreed. It's as though those in charge want it to fail in order to justify an academy.

Then came grim news indeed. Edison, the big American supplier of private education, was coming in. Staff were told that Edison would be interviewing some of them. Edison was founded in 1994 by advertising man Chris Whittle. Whittle also created a television network called Channel One which offered impoverished US schools what appeared to be a bargain. They would each get free use of a satellite receiver, videos, televisions and a public address system. In return they promised to force pupils to watch a ten-minute current affairs broadcast each day, with two minutes of advertising in the middle. Pepsi, Reebok, the US military, Twix and Clearasil were prepared to pay $200,000 for a 30-second message to a captive teen market which could not play truant from the consumer society.

Edison first looked at the opportunities that might be available to it in Britain when Blair's first Education Secretary, David Blunkett, proposed to set up Education Action Zones, the first attempt by the Blair Government to get private industry to run state education.

Edison's then chief executive, Benno Schmidt, came to London to have a look. He told Blunkett that one school, or even one Education Action Zone, would not be worth Edison's while. He wanted a string of schools. And he was bothered by the idea that, after three to five years, he might be required to hand his schools back to the local authority.

Education Action Zones were an embarrassing failure and the Government did not have enough on offer to make it worth Schmidt's while bothering, so he went home and I have never heard of him reappearing in Britain, until now. If he is now getting involved in city academies, this probably means that he has been given the assurances he needs. He will have a string of them, and he will not need to worry about the public sector ever taking control again.

Edison's schools are not the successes that the apostles of privatized education would have you believe. The American Federation of Teachers says: 'In 14 out of 20 states where the company operates, Edison schools performed below average compared to public schools.'

Staff at Islington Green have pointed out that the academy has not yet been agreed, so it is too early to be talking to Edison's emissaries. In October, Ken Muller organized a secret ballot of all staff at the school, and sent the results to the Liberal Democrat Islington Council Executive member for Children's Services, Ursula Wooley, with a covering letter:

Dear Ursula

In the past it has been suggested that the NUT's opposition
to Islington Green School being closed has been unrepresen-
tative of staff feelings. Yesterday's secret ballot of all staff at
the school shows that this is not true. Asked if they agreed
with IGS becoming an academy, this was the response:

Total staff: 120
No: 89 (94.7 per cent of those voting on 78 per cent
turnout)
Yes: 3
Abstentions: 2

Surely this vote by the people responsible for educating
Islington Green students should make you reconsider your
academy plans, which in any case run contrary to your party's
national policy.

If they don't, perhaps you should also take into account the
significantly improved GCSE and SATs results achieved by the
school this year. At the council Executive meeting in July, you
justified recommending a closure notice on IGS on the
grounds that modest improvements made several years ago
had stalled (and I must say that I thought then such a disingenuous misrepresentation was not worthy of you). The rise in
the number of students achieving five A–C GCSEs this year
from 27 to 40 per cent – the fastest in the borough – should, if
you are honest, convince you that Islington Green *is* making
commendable progress and should not be jeopardized by what
your Liberal Democrat national spokespeople have called an
unproven and socially divisive drive to undermine locally
accountable, comprehensive state education.

Already, we have seen 14 jobs being cut and a consequent rise in class sizes this year in order to clear the school's financial deficit in time for it to become an academy in 2008. Now we are told a permanent head teacher cannot be appointed until then either. The real interests of the school and its pupils are being sacrificed so that you can satisfy Lord Adonis and circumvent his veiled threats to withhold funding for Building Schools for the Future if you don't comply with his policy of setting up what are effectively Tory city technology colleges.

IGS staff, many of whom are parents of Islington children, call on you to pull back before it 's too late and you unleash the full force of the educational free market in the borough to the disadvantage of the majority of local kids who don't have the resources required to manipulate an increasingly diverse and unequal school system.

Averre-Beason will not be replaced. The council intends to appoint a temporary head. A permanent head will not be appointed until the school becomes an academy, which at the time of writing could easily be two years away. This leaves the school with a fatal sense of transience, as though there is no future to work for. It may have the effect – it may even be intended to have the effect – of undoing all the good work of recent years.

One has to have a little sympathy for Ursula Woolley and her colleagues, the Liberal Democrat councillors. They know they are flying in the face of their own beliefs, their party's beliefs, and their promises to the electorate. But if they do not do it, the Government will starve their schools of cash.

For it looks as though Government forces have decided on a scorched-earth policy. If Islington Green School is successful, so that there is no case for replacing it with an academy, then that success must be destroyed.

The date for the academy, meanwhile, has been put back to 2008 and possibly 2009. Islington council's assistant director of education met the staff and was told that many of them would leave rather than work in an academy. 'I wouldn't do that, there are many teachers out there ready to take your jobs,' he told them. At the start of November 2006, the governors of Islington Green School, having been told the strength of feeling among the teachers, reversed their position and called for a delay to the closure. The council rushed out a press statement the next day, announcing that the closure notice was to be issued at once.

Muller says: 'There is a danger that academies will create a two-tier system of education to the disadvantage of less well off families.' He points to reports in the *Islington Gazette* that parents hoping to get their children into another, soon-to-be opened Islington academy, St Mary Magdalene, are inundating local estate agents, seeking to buy homes inside the school's catchments area. 'How many local working-class parents will be wealthy enough to do this?' he asks.

Muller hopes for the governors to take a strong line; he hopes for one Liberal defection on the council, which would be enough, in a tight political spot; he hopes that the Labour group will hold firm, and resist inevitable pressure from their party's national leaders. But the odds are stacked against him.

Islington Green School is perhaps the only school in the country to have felt the wrath of the Government not once, but twice. It recovered from Chris Woodhead's decision in 1997. The jury is out on whether it can survive this one.

Note

1. Mark Smulian, *Local Government Chronicle*, 17 February 2005.

8

The Schools that Fail to Fail

'Academies will replace schools which are either in special measures or underachieving,' said David Blunkett when he unveiled the scheme.

Sometimes they do. Sometimes the schools they replace really are the dreadful, rotting, underfunded, undisciplined wrecks that academy propaganda paints. The wreckage, however, is not normally due to the lack of a rich business-person to sprinkle entrepreneurial gold dust over its manage-ment systems, but to lack of money. And quite often, good, well-run schools have been forcibly closed, over the desperate protests of parents.

We saw in the previous chapter how this happened in Isling-ton. But all over the country, good schools have been rubbished, and good teachers seen their careers trashed, to make way for academies. And once they are up and running, academies some-times start to wreck nearby schools.

The north London borough of Brent had one of the first three academies to be announced, and it still contains several angry and embittered former teachers, casualties of the Govern-ment's determination to create city academies.

The justification for creating an academy was that it replaced a failing school. Unless there was a shortage of school places in Brent – and there was not – it was therefore necessary to show that at least one local school had failed. This was urgent because Brent was one of the very few places where the Government had a sponsor, ready and willing, and with £1.5 million, which, while not the £2 million required, was, Mr Blunkett must have calculated, an awful lot better than nothing. It was to specialize in sport, for no particular reason other than that its wealthy sponsor, Sir Frank Lowe, was, in addition to being chairman of Lowe Group, also chairman of Octagon Sports Marketing. He is now Sir Frank.

So Government spin doctors turned their fire on the unfortunate Willesden High School, in a fast and energetic effort to make everyone think it was a failing school. The school had had its troubles, mainly generated by ever-changing Government policy, but by general consent it had emerged from them well, in all the circumstances. Its troubles began when other schools in the area went grant-maintained, because the Conservative Government was offering extra money to do so. Willesden High School stayed with the local authority, and in the 1990s the Conservative-run Brent council cut its funding ruthlessly. Local parents naturally wanted to get their children into the better funded schools. Willesden High School struggled with crumbling buildings.

'From 1997 to 2003, we taught the pupils who could not get in anywhere else, because other schools were effectively selecting,' says Dr Gill Reed, who was a senior teacher there at the time. That meant a high proportion of refugee children. It was quite common for a teacher to be faced with a class of 30, not one of whom had fluent English. And because these children started late in the year, after funding had been allocated, the school got no money for them. 'We were used as a dumping ground', says Dr Reed.

In 1997 the school was placed on special measures because of poor examination results. In those days there was no value-added element in school league tables, and if there had been, the school would have come out in the top 10 per cent in Brent. Dr Reed again: 'Our value-added scores were consistently very good indeed, despite the appalling resources and conditions in which we worked. We welcomed and supported students from all over the world, even though, often, the only resources available were our time and effort.' Nonetheless, says Dr Reed, 'we were named and shamed. But the staff did not leave, as they normally do in failing schools. They stayed, because they knew they were doing a good job.'

In 2000, when Mr Blunkett wanted to close it, the school's examination results were excellent, and much better than the target set by Ofsted. In 2002 it was taken out of special measures. It had a good Ofsted report which concluded: 'The school operates very well in particularly challenging circumstances.' Dr Reed, then a local teaching union leader, was able to write to the council in 2001 on behalf of the teaching unions:

> For much of the past decade, until recently, staff and students have worked in appalling, substandard conditions with inadequate resources. Despite this, in the past four years, Willesden High has managed to achieve outstanding value-added at Key Stage 4. This value-added places Willesden High in the top 5–10 per cent of schools for making good student progress at Key Stage 4.

But by then it had been identified as a place where the city academy experiment might thrive. The proposal was to close Willesden High School on 31 August 2003 and to establish a new city academy on the site the very next day.

In theory, parents were consulted. In practice, they were offered two alternatives: a city academy, or a takeover by the Church of England – this in a school where two-thirds of the pupils are Muslims. For the next year, the school was forced to operate in its crumbling building while watching the city academy being built on its grounds. Its results continued to improve. In its first year the city academy's results were fairly good – but no better, says Dr Reed, than she would have expected. 'Some years were better than others, and they inherited a rather good year from us.'

In Newcastle upon Tyne an academy is due to replace West Gate Community College in September 2008. This is a pretty miserable reward for the work of head teacher Jim Farnie, who in four years has turned the school round. In 2004 about a third of his pupils achieved A–C grades at GCSE, compared with just 8 per cent when he arrived.

Newcastle's Councillors do not want an academy. In fact, the Liberal Democrat council was elected specifically on a platform of not having one. They have made no secret of the reason they changed their minds. Building Schools for the Future money was tied to the academy. If they denied the Government its academy, they would get no money for the city's schools. If they agreed, they could have £200 million.

Councillor Nick Cott, executive member for education, said: 'It's not just the academy that rests on that but the funding for the BSF project. The academy issue has become absolutely linked with BSF. If you want BSF then you have to have an academy.'

*   *   *

Once they are there, the charge against academies is that they damage other local schools. If you pump £20–£30 million into one school, and almost nothing into its neighbours, then you are condemning its neighbours to a version of the poverty trap: people want to go to the other school, so its funding gets even worse, so even more people want to go to the other school, and within a few years you have created yet another failing school.

Of course this is not an invariable pattern. Some academy sponsors allow their schools to work well with their neighbours. And Lesley King, director of Academy Networks at the SSAT, insists that there are other ways in which her organization helps other schools.

She told me: 'Of course the academies programme is a high-profile initiative aimed at 200 schools in the first instance. But this does not mean that other schools are neglected. For instance, here at the SSAT we are engaged with many, through large-scale initiatives such as Raising Achievement Transforming Learning, and we expect to work with many more. We are determined that no school will be left behind.' Determined she may well be, but as long as the SSAT is promoting a system which divides schools into rich and poor, it will be assisting in the creation of sink schools.

Academies are not just destroying good schools, but harming good sixth-form colleges too. Most academies have sixth forms – but many of the schools replaced by academies had no sixth form. 'London colleges', says Julian Gravatt, director of funding and development at the Association of Colleges, 'are facing the challenge of academies that offer specialist 16–18 courses, with a ton of government money and some private sector support.'

Brookhouse College in Hackney was set up to provide comprehensive sixth-form work in an area where the schools were 11–16. The idea was that Brookhouse would provide the sixth form for all of them. But after that, three city academies were approved. They decided to have sixth forms. So other schools felt forced to create sixth forms, believing that, otherwise, they would lose out on the 11-year-olds. Parents were likely to prefer to send their children to a school with a sixth form.

Already, according to one recently retired sixth-form college principal, two colleges near London have been told they will have to merge to remain viable. The retired principal, who asked not to be named, said:

> Sixth-form colleges may well find these more generously funded new institutions undermining their viability and long-term future. City academies are in another realm of funding, and are semi-independent schools. They are bound to have catastrophic effects on other schools struggling on funding provided through local authority and LSC channels. New 'failing' schools will thus be created as the academies cream an area.

Julian Gravatt says:

> The expansion of sixth-form provision from academies will happen at the point (2009) where the 16–18 population begins to fall. If academy sixth forms concentrate on academic A-levels, then they'll be adding to a crowded field. The Learning and Skills Council strategic area reviews (2003–5) showed that there was generally an oversupply of A-level places around the country.

In the same year that academies started, 2000, the Government also created the Learning and Skills Council, to plan 16–19 education, bringing colleges, schools and training providers under one umbrella. But academies are, of course, outside this system, and can do what they like. It is an odd irony – and an example of amazingly unjoined-up government – that in the same year, a system should be created to plan for 16–19 education, and another system created which was bound to wreck such planning.

Says Gravatt:

The Government has planted academies in areas where colleges already operate. It has encouraged them to acquire sixth forms. Their sixth-form funding come directly from the DfES and they are free to operate entirely outside Learning and Skills Council control. Meanwhile, college funding has been tightly squeezed in recent years.

So far, the impact of academies on colleges has been limited to specific areas. In Middlesbrough, the opening of two academies with sixth forms has helped undermine a tertiary system and encouraged other schools to open sixth forms. The net result is more institutions chasing the same number of 16-year-olds. Ultimately there may be fewer course choices. In London, there are academies with vocational facilities duplicating what is available in nearby colleges. The difference is that it is on a smaller scale and without the strength in depth. As the programme expands in the next five years towards the target of 200, academies will have a much larger impact on the 16–19 landscape.

Attempts have been made to transfer the academy model to the college sector in the form of skills academies. Philip Green has put up £12 million to set up a Fashion Retail Academy which will get its running costs largely covered by the Government. Green, a billionaire businessman who owns some of Britain's largest retailers, is Britain's fourth richest man, and lives in tax exile in Monte Carlo.

Two colleges have shown interest so far in sponsoring academies. This is, of course, very odd, because colleges are public sector institutions, and their money is public money. If they produce the sponsor's £2 million, there is no private sector money at all coming in, which seems to negate the whole purpose. But that is the topsy-turvy world in which we are living.

9

Selecting Staff, Sponsors and Students

If failure sometimes has to be induced so that the school can be closed to make way for an academy, this cannot be said of Bexley City Academy. No one seems to have a kind word to say for the late unlamented Thamesmead School. Words used in the same breath tend to be vandalism, graffiti and truanting. Here was a school that really did need to be replaced with something better.

And if some academy sponsors have failed to win hearts and minds locally – Sir Peter Vardy springs to mind – this cannot entirely be said of Bexley sponsor Sir David Garrard. Local journalist Linda Piper of the *Bromley News Shopper* tells a story of how he was told that some parents were going to struggle to pay for the expensive, and compulsory, uniform, so he quietly set up a five-figure fund to help them. Piper is impressed. 'It's in another league from what went before, it's raised aspirations and the kids there have no problem with wearing a uniform that identifies them as business academy pupils.'

'I have seen the future of education, and this is it', said Tony Blair when he opened the Bexley Business Academy in 2003. 'When I look at this school, and see the pupils, parents, teachers and those who have made it all happen, I know why I am in politics.'

But two years later Ofsted rated as 'inadequate' Bexley's overall effectiveness, the effectiveness of its sixth form, the quality of teaching and learning, the sixth-form curriculum, the care, guidance and support given to sixth formers, and leadership and management in the sixth form. Ofsted has four grades: outstanding, good, satisfactory and inadequate. The academy got 'inadequate' or 'satisfactory' under all headings.

There is a persistent rumour that the inspectors told head teacher Tom Widdows they were going to fail the school, and place it in special measures; and that they were persuaded not to do so. It is not true: the school obtained retractions from those newspapers which repeated the rumour. Such rumours are bound to circulate after the Islington Green episode described in Chapter 7. The school didn't fail, but it was touch and go.

Bexley was built to replace a failing secondary school – but also two successful primary schools which the parents fought, unsuccessfully, to save. It has so far cost a staggering £58.2 million, and some original design mistakes still have to be put right. Classrooms were built with three walls, the fourth wall being absent, on the theory that it would aid classroom discipline, but it has done the opposite, and the fourth wall will now be filled in.

Sir Norman Foster was hired to design it, naturally. Though without experience of designing schools, he has proved the academy sponsors' favourite architect, and has designed no fewer than five of them. It's safe to suppose that if a public body – say a local council – was building a school and going many million of pounds over budget, it would get a somewhat less sympathetic hearing from the Government than Sir David got. He wanted business at the heart of his academy. Sir Norman's design is therefore dominated by a huge replica stock market trading floor in the centre of the building, to remind the students of what really matters in life, which is of course making oodles of money. And the National Curriculum is crammed into four days, so that Friday can be spent entirely on business and enterprise. The children spend the day setting up their own businesses.

The BBC's Gerry Northam described what this was like in *File on 4* on 23 November 2004: 'Inside the main entrance is a large open space with the school's own Stock Exchange at the centre, where the head of Business and Economics, Hassan Noor, in his first teaching job, is struggling to make himself heard against the racket coming from the open cafeteria.'

Hassan Noor was heard on Northam's report beginning his class: 'Today we're going to be talking about the wealth effects that originate from stock markets. David, can you start us off? If there's a rise in share prices that creates wealth effects. What kind of effect do you think that has on the economy?' David replied: 'It'll increase spending in the economy and it'll make people feel that they're richer.' Gerry Northam commented: 'The response of the students is a model of entrepreneurial vision, in line with the academy's motto: "No Goal Is Beyond Our Reach".'

Head teacher Tom Widdows reached for an Alastair Campbell-patented phrase when justifying to Northam what he was doing. 'If we want to break away from bog-standard education, then we need to do things differently', he said.

Sir David, having no experience of education, asked one of the mushrooming educational consultancies to run the school. He chose 3Es, the firm set up by the first head of the first city technology college, Valerie Bragg, and the late Stanley Goodchild, a former chief education officer for Berkshire. Tony Blair, opening the academy, made a point of crediting them: 'Stanley Goodchild and Valerie Bragg, for their educational leadership of the academy project through their path-breaking company 3Es. 3Es apparently stands for "education, education, education". I've heard that phrase somewhere before, and am wondering whether they should be paying royalties.'

The Prime Minister's endorsement will have helped 3Es win

the contracts they now have for four more academies in Chelsea, Lewisham, Croydon and Liverpool; but this is hardly a surprise, since Valerie Bragg is also an adviser to the Prime Minister's office on regeneration of schools.

3Es, like Sir David himself, has an attitude towards employing teachers and towards the teaching trade unions which might politely be described as robust. At the start, when the representatives of two teaching unions went to see Mr Widdows and his senior management team, they had a courteous hearing and reached general agreement on most points, including union representation. But when it had not been implemented six months later, and they enquired about it, it turned out that the governors, with their inbuilt majority of sponsor nominees, had not yet considered it. They have still not approved it, three years on, and the teaching unions are not recognized. The school's head and his senior staff were willing enough, so has union recognition been vetoed by Sir David's people and 3Es?

The result is some very bitter employment experiences. Local union representatives say the academy is employing people with 30 years' teaching experience on six-month contracts. An experienced woman teacher was attacked by a teenage male pupil and thrown round the room. She tried to keep coming to work, but found it impossible seeing the pupil who had attacked her, and also was still at the school. So she stayed away for a while longer to try to recover her nerve. Then she found that, because she was on a six-month contract, she only had five days' sick pay.

No wonder that Ofsted reported: 'Recruitment and retention of staff has been difficult. There is a high turnover of teaching staff and a large number of the teachers are relatively inexperienced . . . Most of the senior leaders have been in their posts for a maximum of two terms and some only started at the beginning of this term.'

City academies, and especially those which concentrate on business, are under enormous pressure to do something different, or (to use the politically correct term) innovative. None of them has yet made children learn while standing on their heads, to improve the flow of blood to their brains, but pretty well everything else has been tried. At Bexley, apart from the business Friday described above, there are several experiments going on, and these and their results have been described by a member of staff who wants to remain anonymous:

> Students are never allowed a break outside of the school. They must stay in the building all day.
>
> Students are given two half-hour 'brunch' breaks. These are not at the same time as other students. These breaks are staggered throughout the day, from 9.30 a.m. to 2 p.m., so that different groups are together. Brunch takes place in a large room without windows. Students have no opportunity to let off steam and are constantly monitored. This causes considerable problems, as the inspectors discovered. Any students who have complained have basically been told that they are lucky to be in the academy and should shut up. It has been nicknamed the 'Belmarsh Academy' (after the local prison) as a result.

A parent, Clare Wood, made the same point in a local newspaper, the *Bromley News Shopper*:

> There is no playground; nowhere for a bunch of unruly 11–16-year-olds to let off steam. Even the prisoners at Belmarsh get an hour to enjoy the horrendous stench of Thamesmead. My son is, thankfully, in his final year at this institution, that is failing dismally in its Dickensian approach

> to young people . . . I am now threatened with a phone call
> from my son's teacher who discovered him outside the
> building. Summer approaches, and these children are forbid-
> den to go outside for the entire day . . . Can someone please
> let these children play?

The idea, apparently, is to prevent bullying, which was endemic
in the predecessor school. If the children are constantly inside,
supervised, and groups have breaks at different times, the theory
is that there will be less bullying. But it does mean that energy
and aggression are bottled up.

The staff member continued: '3Es work on a system of high
turnover of staff. They are paranoid about power blocs developing in subjects, and use the flat structure to prevent leaders
emerging.' Tom Widdows put the same point like this: 'The
most controversial thing I have done is not to have heads of
departments or years. Those jobs are shared between the
teachers, who phone the parents directly with updates of their
children, good and bad.'

The staff member adds: 'The lack of trade unions and the
staggered day means staff rarely have any contact with each
other.'

There is no doubt that Bexley Academy's results are better
than those of the struggling school it replaced, though not (as
the Ofsted report made clear) as much of an improvement as
they should be. It has a new start, in the most expensive school
building in the land. If it was freed of Sir David's obsession with
turning children into little entrepreneurs, the restless experi-
mentation of 3Es, and a management style which seems
designed to tame the teacher unions and make teachers like
private sector employees, it could perhaps be doing much
better.

In January 2005 head Tom Widdows told the *Guardian*: 'I am now the longest-serving head of a city academy in the country. To my knowledge no other principal has lasted more than six months, and I have been here three years.' He was right: the turnover of city academy head teachers has been truly alarming. Alas, he clearly did not know that he himself was to become part of the problem, leaving the job the following year in mysterious circumstances. Rumour in the school is that he fell out with 3Es, and that, left to himself, he might have done quite well. But, of course, no one knows for certain. In an academy, it can all be done secretly, by the sponsor and their advisers.

*   *   *

Mr Widdows joined a fast-growing group of former academy heads. In September 2004 the fourth head of the Greig Academy in Haringey started work. By then it was clear that there was a spectacularly high turnover of head teachers in academies. Getting and keeping good heads seemed beyond academy sponsors.

And getting and keeping good teachers was even harder. Teachers in academies are outside all the negotiated national agreements. The academy must make its own deals, and some academy sponsors feel a mission to show how much tougher and more demanding a private sector employer can be than the public sector teachers are used to dealing with. This leads to a lot of posturing, which wastes both time and motivation.

But it is, it seems, what the Government wants. Ministers have said that sponsors, though most have no experience of education, should be closely involved with the leadership of the school. It is not surprising that consultants PricewaterhouseCoopers, in a

Government-commissioned report, found 'problems with work-force development, especially on how to strike a balance between new and existing staff'.

The House of Commons Select Committee on Education reported in 2005 that the role of sponsor was not at all clear. 'What does a sponsor add to a school? Do they stimulate improvement above and beyond that of a school which is not sponsored?'

The MPs on the committee tried the questions on Charles Clarke when he was Education Secretary, and this is the answer they got:

> If you go through most of the academies so far, you will see a significant education improvement, even by comparison with the predecessor school, in each of those areas. The education benefit is the engagement of the sponsor who is really trying to take it forward . . . I would argue – and this goes back to research conducted literally decades ago – that it is the leadership ethos structure of the school which determines its results . . . I think the academies are working to that end and the involvement of the external sponsor has helped that to happen in quite significant ways.

Leaving aside the probably unanswerable question of what a 'leadership ethos structure' is when it's at home, Mr Clarke's answer only begged more questions. For, said the Select Committee, most sponsors have no background in education, so just how should they operate? 'Should they be involved in day-to-day management of the school, which is normally a matter for the head teacher? Does the sponsor bear any accountability if the school fails? If so, to whom is he or she accountable, and how?'

Of course the reality is that the sponsor can be involved as much or as little as he or she wishes. The sponsor is paying the piper (though with public money) and can call the tune. A sponsor who wants to be in and out, helping, advising – as, say, Alec Reed does – can do that. A sponsor who wants to lay down the design of the building, like Sir David Garrard, can do that; and a sponsor who is most interested in ensuring that his or her particular religious views are taught (Sir Peter Vardy, Robert Edmiston) can do that. Whatever their views about education, these can be reflected. Mr Edmiston says his views are 'traditional'. We will see a lot of children learning in serried rows in Solihull, then.

'We agree', said the Select Committee, 'that the participation of an enthusiastic and committed private sponsor might benefit a school. But, once again, the DfES does not seem to have set up a rigorous enough structure to evaluate the effects of sponsorship. It might be prudent to establish a number of academies without sponsors so that the effect of sponsorship can be properly monitored and tested, or to examine the role of sponsorship of different characters in CTCs.'

*   *   *

The Select Committee also worried about whether 'the good results achieved by some Academies may have come at the price of excluding those children that are harder to teach and reducing the proportion of children in the school from deprived backgrounds (whom they were originally intended to serve)'.

We have already seen that some academies make use of their power to exclude children far more easily than state schools (and force the despised state sector to take them). A 2004 study by Professor Stephen Gorard of York University found that the

King's and Unity Academies in Middlesbrough had expelled 61 pupils between them since the start of the school year in 2002, compared with 15 from all other secondary schools in the borough. Professor Gorard also found that the number of students entitled to free school meals at Unity was 47 per cent, compared with nearly 60 per cent at its predecessor school.

Some academies use their power to select 10 per cent of their intake on aptitude for the specialism. Many do not: neither the Oasis Trust, nor Sir Peter Vardy's Emmanuel Schools Foundation, two evangelical Christian sponsors, use their power to select 10 per cent of the entry.

The method of selection varies. Each academy has its own method, decided by the sponsor, cleared with the Government (it has to conform to national guidelines), and contained in the funding agreement.

Everything depends on the sponsor. Some behave with scrupulous fairness. The Oasis Trust – the first of whose five academies will open in September 2007 – insists on using exactly the same entrance procedures as the local authority. Its founder and chief executive, Steve Chalke, would have liked to call their academies 'community schools' but Lord Adonis would not allow him to do so. Nor will Oasis pay heads and teachers any differently from other heads and teachers in the area. Unlike many academy sponsors, Mr Chalke has talked to the teaching trade unions and negotiated what a local union representative has called 'acceptable' pay and conditions. Mr Chalke fears impoverishing neighbouring schools. 'It's about creating choice for people who have been robbed of choice', he says. 'We are rigorous that we do not create a great school at the expense of other local schools.'

This view is rooted in Mr Chalke's own childhood. An 11-plus failure, he knows that if you go to the area's sink school, 'it's like having to put on a badge saying, I failed to get into the good school'.

But he does not have to do this. Other sponsors behave very differently from the Oasis Trust. 'Academies are not required to conform to local admissions arrangements; they are their own admissions forums' reports the NUT's *Academies: Looking Beyond the Spin*. 'There is a wide diversity of practice regarding admissions in academies including entrance tests, various forms of banding, sibling places, random selection such as lotteries, as well as selection by aptitude. The criterion of home-to-school distance used by academies also varies.'

Several use a system known as banding. An entry test is set, and potential pupils divided into, say, four ability bands. The same proportion of pupils is then accepted from each band. This, in an area of high deprivation, can skew the intake towards the higher ability range, and against local children. If your school is right beside a particularly deprived estate, you are likely to find that a very large proportion of the children come into the lowest band, because their educational opportunities have been severely limited for the first 11 years of their lives. If this happens, then the lowest band will fill very fast, and the school will go further afield for pupils to fill the allocations in the higher bands.

The NUT booklet says:

There is evidence to suggest that academies are seeking to attract more academically successful pupils. For the Bristol Academy, expensive leaflets advertising the academy were distributed in only the more affluent areas. One of the first academies to open, Greig in Haringey, targeted leafy suburbs several miles away, rather than the neighbourhead area which was severely deprived.

In July 2005 the *TES* reported figures showing that most (not all) academies had fewer deprived pupils than the schools they replaced and more from outside the local area. In eight out of 13 academies that had directly replaced schools, the proportion of disadvantaged pupils had decreased. In March 2006 *Children Now* magazine showed that there was a drop in the number of special needs children in academies compared with predecessor schools.

The NUT's Ken Muller points to some unexpected figures for the number of children eligible for free school meals in schools in Hackney, east London. Mossbourne Academy, he says, is surrounded by deprived council estates. Yet the figures are: Haggerston 57 per cent, Clapton Girls 52 per cent, Homerton 50 per cent, Stoke Newington 40 per cent – and Mossbourne 37 per cent. 'What looks like a fair system actually discriminates against local working-class children', says Muller.

If there is any sort of covert selection, then, given that the splendid new school upon which a fortune has been spent is bound to be more attractive than existing cash-starved schools, it will not just skew the results: it will send neighbouring schools into a cycle of decline. In addition to having less money and poorer buildings and facilities, they will also be teaching mostly the academy's rejects. They will, inevitably, have poorer results, and start to be seen as sink schools. The academies, insofar as they succeed at all, will be succeeding by ensuring the failure of other schools.

So the House of Commons Select Committee said:

We are concerned that the effect of academies on nearby schools should be monitored. Where new academies are established, the local school place planning process needs to be carefully managed in order to prevent any adverse effects on existing schools. For example, if a new academy draws pupils away from existing schools, those schools will suffer a reduction in funding and may have to reduce staffing levels as a result. In addition, it is intended that all academies will have sixth forms. This may result in well-qualified teachers from nearby schools without sixth forms moving to academies, creating recruitment problems in those schools.

The monitoring the committee asked for has not happened. Here is the best I can find by way of answer from the Government – a reply given to a journalist by a DfES press officer:

> It's worth pointing out though that academies have many of the characteristics of schools which have higher than average exclusion rates nationally – high numbers of free school meals, low levels of pupil achievement, etc. Records from predecessor schools are also unreliable and exclusions are likely to be under-reported. Some academies also have many more pupils than their predecessor schools, so the overall number of exclusions can be higher.
>
> However, anecdotally, it seems that academies do reduce the number of exclusions in their second year. Greig reduced its fixed term exclusions from 166 to 28 in its second year of opening and its permanent exclusions fell from 12 to two. At Unity (in Middlesbrough) the number of permanent exclusions fell from 23 to 14. So there does seem to be a downwards trend.

*   *   *

The process of improving and gentrifying the academy intake reached its logical conclusion in 2006 when it was announced that two private fee-charging school are soon to become academies. It is just worth reminding ourselves at this point that the academy scheme was sold to us as a way of improving standards in the poorest inner-city areas, for the poorest children; and that they were to replace decaying and failing inner-city schools.

Now, however, the Government is to hand up to £6 million to the United Learning Trust (ULT) to turn William Hulme's Grammar School in Manchester (fees £8,148 a year) into an academy with a languages specialism. It will select 10 per cent of its pupils on aptitude for languages.

This is how it happened. Stephen Patriarca, the energetic and resourceful head teacher, was struggling to survive in an area over-supplied with fee-charging schools. He had to compete with at least three others, all with good reputations. Parents at his school are typically not particularly rich – they include Manchester taxi drivers, seven out of ten of his pupils are from ethnic minorities and four out of ten are Muslims. Projections were not good: the school age population in the area is set to fall dramatically.

His first thought was to get more bursaries. But then he was introduced to Lord Adonis, who opened up a whole new future for him as a city academy.

The school will keep its elegant old buildings, and £6 million will be spent on new buildings to increase pupil numbers. ULT will raise some sponsorship money, but the lion's share of the £6 million will come from the Government.

ULT is a Christian educational charity which runs ten private fee-charging schools, and is also the biggest academy sponsor. It aims to bring the state and private sectors of education together.

Mr Patriarca says: 'We are different from other ULT academies because we are not denominational. I drafted the religious studies policy, and we teach Islam as the main religion here.

They have agreed to that.' A spokesman for ULT emphasized to me that they do not bar non-Christian pupils anywhere, not even in their private fee-charging schools.

Mr Patriarca told the *Guardian*'s Donald MacLeod that he expects the new academy to become a 'flagship' for academies.

> The problem with the academies programme is that many have replaced seriously failing schools and the improvements they have made are not always appreciated because they are starting from such a low base. The Government wants to see some academies based on highly successful schools. We are looking to establish the school as a centre for excellence for teaching and learning for the academies programme. We are not talking about becoming a local authority comprehensive.

What about selection? The school currently has an entrance examination, though Mr Patriarca has been forced to lower the bar over the years because of the competition from other local fee-charging schools, and it is now not highly selective. So it will be no great shock to the system to be reduced to selecting only 10 per cent, and taking in the rest on a banding system. 'There's a challenge here for independent schools', says Mr Patriarca. 'We say we are so good, and now the government is challenging us to show that we can be successful with a mixed ability intake.' But when it comes to the sixth form, there will be no messing about: it will select by ability.

The other fee-charging school set to become an academy is Belvedere, a girls' school in Liverpool. This is one of the schools where Sir Peter Lampl's Sutton Trust and the Girls' Day School Trust have jointly been paying for places for bright children on a needs-blind basis. For seven years, the Sutton Trust has sponsored more than 70 per cent of the school's intake. A third of the intake have had free places because the family income is less than £14,000, and the rest of the sponsored students have paid fees on a sliding scale according to income.

Sir Peter wanted the Government to adopt this scheme. He disliked the academies project because it meant concentrating too much money on too few children. However, the Government made it clear that it was an academy or nothing.

Belvedere, like William Hulme, will cost much less than a normal academy. On that basis Sir Peter has agreed – with a good deal of reluctance – to be co-sponsor along with the Girls' Day School Trust, paying between them 10 per cent of the £7 million capital cost of the scheme. And this academy will become, to a great extent, a selective school. The sixth form will be massively expanded, to the point where eventually it will constitute about half the school. And the sixth form will be selective.

The city academy programme, billed as new schools, replacing failing schools, without selection, teaching the country's most underprivileged children, has strayed a long way. Where will it go next?

10

But Does It Work?

It's easy to sneer, but does it work, as Tony Blair might have said
– and probably has.

So let's forget for a moment what academies do to other
schools and colleges and the communities in which they
operate, and concentrate on what they do for those who attend
them. Are they an improvement?

They had better be. If you spend between £35 million and
£50 million of public money on building a school, instead of
the £20 million or so a new school normally costs; if you insist
on a new building in a school which, according to Sir Peter
Lampl, often only needs refurbishment; and if a pupil at that
school costs the taxpayer nearly twice as much to educate as a
pupil at ordinary schools, you need to show they are a cut above
the rest.

Can they show better results? Are the expensive buildings an
improvement on the cheap ones erected by cash-starved local
councils? What do parents and pupils think?

Are the results better?

Sometimes. It's hard to be sure what is going on, since statistics
on results can often be presented to prove diametrically
opposite things.

The trade union Unison, in its 2005 booklet *Academies Called
to Account*, looked closely at results. It found that of the 11

academies listed in the 2004 GCSE tables, five showed no improvement and one had the second-worst results in England. In the league tables of 14-year-olds' tests' results published in March 2005, nine of 11 academies were in the bottom 200 schools in England. The other six academies in existence at the time were not included in the results. In the 2005 GCSE league tables, seven of the 14 academies remain in the bottom 200 schools. The 2004 GCSE results of 14 academies showed improvement in ten and a worsening of results for the remaining four.

One of these four was Unity City Academy in Middlesbrough, which failed its Ofsted inspection and was in special measures. West London Academy, too, failed its Oftsed inspection. Bexley Business Academy had a very poor Ofsted report in November 2005, teetering on the brink of failure, which said: 'Teaching and learning are inadequate overall.'

It is worth pausing for a moment to consider the implications of the fact that, in its first years, the academy programme has produced two failing schools and one near failure.

When an ordinary school fails its inspection, it finds ministers on its back at once, demanding that the local council should hand control to a private company (and, probably, replace the school with an academy). The head will be unceremoniously dumped and replaced with a so-called superhead. Journalists will be briefed on how an ever-vigilant government is saving our young people from this failing school and its incompetent managers. But in the case of the Unity City Academy, the Government quietly bunged the school a few million more pounds to help it recover. Neighbouring schools struggling to keep up standards on desperately stretched budgets were not amused.

However, there have been achievements. The PricewaterhouseCoopers (PWC) report commissioned by the Government, looking at the three academies which opened in 2002, found that two, the business academy in Bexley and Greig City Academy in Haringey, had significantly improved results (the third was Unity City Academy).

The PWC report was suppressed by the Government, and then, when they were forced to unveil it (the *Times Educational Supplement* used the Freedom of Information Act), ministers hailed it as a vindication, though it also contained serious reservations. The local authority pressure group The Education Network (TEN) thinks PWC fell into a Government trap of using misleading data. TEN says that the comparisons in the report and the department's response are made with national average figures rather than schools with similar characteristics. The latter, it claims, would have been more meaningful. It accuses the Government of 'disingenuous use' of selective data.

TEN pointed to a programme involving a group of the lowest-performing London schools which increased their GCSE performance by 4.5 points last year, at a cost of £3 million a year for 68 schools. Each individual academy costs about ten times that sum.

January 2006 brought some seriously bad news for academies. Half of them were named among the worst-performing schools in England, in league tables published for every state and private secondary school ranking their results in 2005's GCSE exams.

Of the 14 which had been open long enough for their 2005 GCSE results to be included in the rankings, seven were in the bottom 200 using the benchmark of the proportion of pupils gaining five or more passes at grades A*–C. Fewer than 30 per cent of the pupils attending these seven academies gained five C grades or better.

At the flagship Bexley Business Academy in Kent, only 29 per cent achieved five or more good GCSEs, while at the Capital City Academy in Brent, north London, and Unity City Academy in Middlesbrough, just 16 per cent of pupils achieved this benchmark.

A spokeswoman for the Department for Education and Skills made the best of a bad job: 'Academies are continuing to make strong increases in the numbers of their pupils getting five or more good GCSEs', she said, adding that GCSE results for academies overall had increased at three times the national average.

The average five A*–C GCSE results of the 14 open academies was approximately 36.4 per cent in 2005, compared to an average 21 per cent in their predecessor schools in 2002 when the first academies opened. All seven academies have improved GCSE results compared to the very poor results recorded by their predecessor schools in 2002, some of which had only just come out of special measures.

March 2006 saw Ofsted reports on Mossbourne Academy in Hackney, City Academy Bristol, and Walsall Academy. Schools Minister Lord Andrew Adonis hailed them as evidence that the academy programme was 'raising standards, improving exam results and behaviour and helping bring new hope to deprived communities'. He said: 'These Ofsted reports show that academies have done an excellent job in a very short time to turn around a history of educational failure in some of the most deprived areas in the country.'

Well, up to a point. They were all undeniably good reports. The report on Mossbourne Academy in particular was extraordinarily fulsome, and a letter to pupils from the inspectors said: 'Your academy is very special. It has achieved the highest grade that can be awarded to a school; it is outstanding because it gives you a first-class education. You told us that you are proud of your academy and we recognize why you and your parents feel so strongly about everything that it provides.'

Lord Adonis commented: 'Academies are getting results – the average increase across all academies of pupils getting five good GCSE results is nearly 8 per cent, outstripping the national average of 2.6 per cent. Academies transform young lives for the better, and that's why they are popular with parents.'

But this meant rather less than Lord Adonis suggested. The previous year, 2005, the House of Commons Select Committee on Education put academy successes in context. It reported:

> Mr Clarke [Charles Clarke, then Education Secretary] described to the Committee the good results attained by some Academies in comparison with predecessor schools on the same site. He cited the achievements of Bexley Academy, the City Academy, Bristol and King's Academy, Middlesbrough, which have all significantly raised the percentage of pupils attaining five A*–C grades at GCSE. We welcome the success of academies which have raised educational standards in areas of historical underachievement. However, we observe that other academy schools seem not to have produced improved results compared to the school that was previously on their site. Figures published in January 2005 for 11 academies showed that five have not improved performance at GCSE and that in some cases, the percentage achieving five A*–C grades has actually declined.

The Select Committee concluded that the government was racing ahead with the city academy programme without sufficient evidence that it produced better results.

We do not believe that the link between diverse types of schools and improved overall standards has been proven. We have similar concerns regarding both the academy initiative and the Specialist Schools programme. Despite the Government's proclaimed attachment to evidence-based policy, expensive schemes seem to be rolled out before being adequately tested and evaluated compared to other less expensive alternatives.

Where they can be shown to improve results, the improvement is not always what it seems.

Terry Wrigley, educational researcher at Edinburgh University and editor of *Improving Schools*, reported on academies in May 2006. He said some academies were diverting children away from GCSEs to boost their standing in league tables. His study found that many children had been switched from taking separate subjects at GCSE to the vocational qualification GNVQ, which counts as four GCSEs in Government league tables. The proportion of children taking GNVQ has risen from 13 per cent at predecessor schools to 52 per cent at academies.

He compared the first 11 academies in 2005 with their predecessor schools in 2002 on the basis of how many of their pupils got five A*–Cs or equivalent at GCSE. Academies showed a rise of 14 per cent. But if – as the DfES now requires – you say that these GCSEs must include English and maths, the improvement shrank to 0.6 (just over half a percentage point). 'Further analysis showed that almost all of the "improvement" in the academies was in fact due to a switch from GCSE to GNVQ rather than a genuine improvement in standards', writes Dr Wrigley.

He told the *Guardian* on 22 May 2006: 'Of course we should value vocational learning as well as academic learning, but false equivalents simply let down the most vulnerable young people. It may be in the school's short-term interests, and the Government's, to improve exam statistics in this way. However, as soon as an individual applies for a job or university place, they will face problems.'

In March 2006 the *TES* came to a very similar conclusion. It found only a 3 per cent improvement in academies' GCSE results over predecessor schools. Two of the longest opened academies – Greig (Haringey) and Unity (Middlesbrough) – had worse results. And – crucially – when vocational qualifications (GNVQs) were removed, the percentage fell by half in eight of the 14 academies. Walsall Academy fell from 67 per cent getting five A–C grades to seven per cent.

I put in a request for an interview with Lord Adonis, so that I could put all the conflicting evidence to him. Sadly, though I offered him any time he liked over a five-week period, he replied at once that he was unable to find time to meet me. Nor did he answer the questions I was invited to put to him by email. His office sent me his various statements.

These give me his take on the 2005 GCSE results, in which nine of 11 academies were in the bottom 200 schools in England. He says they show

striking improvements for almost all of the new academies . . . The proportion of pupils gaining five or more good GCSEs rose by an average of 6.3 percentage points in academies, which is about four times the usual national average increase; 17 of the 21 academies posted improvements, including nine where results rose by 10 or more percentage points in this year alone . . . The question now is not whether academies succeed, but how many more are needed in future to respond to parental demand.

This year's GCSE results for academies show outstanding improvement. They demonstrate academies to be an immensely worthwhile initiative to bring about more good schools which parents want and where pupils achieve. And parents clearly agree. There are three applications for each academy place this September.

His statement also told me: 'Academies have had to overcome a history of poor performance and low aspirations inherited from predecessor schools . . .' This, in the case of many academies discussed in this book, is simply untrue. I would have liked the chance to ask Lord Adonis for his take on, say, Coulby Newham School in Middlesbrough, discussed in Chapter 5.

He added: 'Pupils once expected to fail are now succeeding – and we are striving to ensure that they achieve at the very highest levels.' Try telling that to Jack and his mother (see Chapter 5). Jack was expected to succeed in one of these much-abused predecessor schools – and is now failing, because the school was closed to make way for an academy.

Research by Professor Stephen Gorard of York University suggests that where academies are raising standards, they are doing it by improving their intake rather than doing better with the same pupils. 'An academy is sometimes unfairly expected to make a big difference very quickly, when turning round a school can take up to five years', says Lesley King, Director of Academy Networks at the SSAT. And that may be true. But they should surely be judged by the same unforgiving standards that ministers apply to 'bog-standard' state comprehensives, especially since they have had preferential treatment.

There is no doubt that some, though not all, of the academies have improved results, though trying to quantify the improvement would simply get us into a statistical quagmire. It seems likely that these improved results would have occurred as a result of the extra public investment, without the assistance of sponsors. And a few – Unity in Middlesbrough being the most obvious example – have entirely, inexplicably and unforgivably failed to raise standards, despite all the financial and other advantages they have been given over their predecessor schools and over neighbouring schools.

Do the buildings work?

If you spend a lot of money on a brand-new school building, then, for the first year or two, it will have a good effect on everyone connected with it – pupils, parents, teachers, other staff. It would have to be a spectacularly incompetent design if it failed to do this. And many academies have seen benefits from this, in terms of pupil behaviour, motivation, morale, and (sometimes) attainment.

But academy buildings have come under fire from a most surprising quarter, and one we have to take seriously: the man charged with driving the programme forward, Sir Cyril Taylor. He told the *Guardian* in 2005: 'The whole building side has been a nightmare. Most of the 27 already open are OK. There are some outstanding ones, but there are some we shouldn't repeat.'

He attacked the hugely expensive Bexley Business Academy in Kent, designed by Sir Norman Foster, which has so far absorbed an estimated £58 million of public money (new schools are normally reckoned to cost a little over £20 million to build). This is the school of which the Prime Minister said: 'I have seen the future of education, and this is it.' But Sir Cyril called the design 'crazy' and added: 'I would never have built that building. You can't teach in that.' Classrooms at the Bexley

Business Academy have three walls; the fourth wall, behind the students, is open. Sir Cyril told the *Guardian* that the fourth wall is now going to be filled in.

The building is a monument to sponsor Sir David Garrard's concern that the academy should be about business and enterprise, which made him decree that every Friday would be spent on teaching children how to succeed in business, with the core curriculum subjects being squeezed into the other four days. The school is therefore dominated by a huge mock stock market trading floor.

But Bexley was not the only building to arouse Sir Cyril's scorn. 'We're not going to have any more glass palaces', he told the *Guardian*. 'We're going to have functional buildings built of brick. Glass is hot in the summer, freezing in the winter. People can look through it and nasties throw bricks at it. And you don't have balconies on schools, anybody can tell you that.' He promised 'No toilets in nasty dark areas' in future academies.

More temperately, the PWC report said that the 'design of some academies is not practical for modern teaching and learning'. They 'generally have the appearance of modern office buildings or universities, and seek to make bold statements in their local communities'.

The building problems are dismissed by the Government as 'teething troubles'. But it should have predicted what was likely to happen when you say to someone whose life has been spent amassing a fortune in business: 'You have almost unlimited access to public funds, now build a school the way you think it ought to be built.' They will go to the most splendid architect they can find – Sir Norman Foster, who had never built a school before, seems to have been a favourite with academy sponsors – and they will tell him that money is no object. They will give him their priorities – in Sir David Garrard's case a stock market trading floor.

And they will probably tell him to 'think outside the box' or do 'blue skies thinking', or some other bit of dead management jargon. And they will get buildings that are like great triumphalist offices, or aircraft hangars. They will get monuments to the contemporary obsession with money and people who amass it, like Victorian follies. What they will not get is schools.

And they will not get them quickly and efficiently. All the private sector gold dust in the world has not saved the building project at the Paddington Academy, currently delayed for a year because of a contract dispute between the builder and a subcontractor. For this reason, in the 2006–7 academic year, pupils are working in a seriously substandard temporary building, and no one knows who is going to pay the extra half-million pounds over the budget which it is going to cost. The building, advertised on the website with the usual management gush ('a new academy offering exciting and innovative learning experiences') is a building site.

Westminster Council, according to a *Newsnight* report, feels it has shelled out enough money. It is a fair bet that the sponsor, the United Learning Trust, will not feel like picking up the bill. It will be very surprising if it ends up on anyone's desk other than that of Lord Adonis, who has access to apparently unlimited supplies of taxpayers' money with which to rescue academies that go wrong.

Newsnight reporter Paul Mason asked the obvious question:

The purpose of bringing in private sector expertise is to make things work better. Clearly in this case they have not. With so much personal kudos invested in academies by top Labour ministers, is there a danger that third sector suppliers come to believe there is no effective penalty for failure?

He wanted to put the question to Lord Adonis. But Lord Adonis could not find time to talk to him, any more than to me.

Does it work?

In the written statement Lord Adonis gave me instead of an interview, he told me: 'Those who question the success of academies should speak to some of the thousands of children being encouraged to reach their potential and do well in life. Academies are making great progress, and the best is yet to come.'

It is true that PricewaterhouseCoopers found that the schools were popular among parents and children, and so were the sponsors and head teachers. It reported 'innovative approaches to curriculum, staffing, teaching and learning, and timetabling, good impact on pupil behaviour, innovative design'.

They have not solved the problems of state education. Bullying, said the report, was a significant problem in some academies, and was at the same level as in state schools.

But by and large, those who attended academies, and their parents, liked what they saw. PWC did not, of course, interview those in the local community whose children attended other schools, nor to pupils like Jack, discussed in Chapter 5, who fell victim to the more draconian exclusions policy in academies, nor to the two in three applicants (on Lord Adonis's figures) who have to attend another, less financially privileged, school because there is no place in the academy. I have tried to put their point of view in some of the other chapters of this book.

In a very limited sense – does it work for those pupils who attend academies, leaving aside the rest of the community in which they live? – the answer is a pretty definite 'Maybe'. Throwing money at a problem does yield results. The improvements are modest, and certainly no more than you would have expected the extra money to buy.

Had the money been spent differently, and not been handed over to private sponsors to spend as they wished, the improvement it bought might have been greater. Had the money been spent more or less evenly among those state schools that needed it, it would have bought more overall benefit. There is no real evidence that the academy model itself has produced any benefits.

Of course, as the PWC report pointed out, we have not yet had time to prove this either way. So it seems to me that the Parliamentary Select Committee was offering modest, sober, sensible advice in 2005 which the Government should have heeded. It said:

The capital cost of academies is significantly beyond that of other new schools. The academies currently in operation generally provide places for around 1,200 students in each school. At an average cost of £25 million per school, this represents a cost of almost £21,000 per place. In contrast, the Government's basic need cost multipliers for building new secondary school accommodation is just under £14,000 per place. It is equally important to note that although academies are planned to take large numbers of pupils eventually, they often begin with small rolls and some build up from a Year 7 only intake in their first year of operation. This increases the cost per pupil far beyond the cost per place.

These figures are not included in the *Five Year Strategy*. Indeed, none of the proposals are costed in that document. Nevertheless, the city academy programme represents a significant investment of public funds, which deserves proper scrutiny. We recognize that secondary education has failed in some inner-city areas and we understand the temptation to believe that academies are the solution. Yet £5 billion is a lot of money to commit to one programme. The Government could have limited the number of Academies to 30 or 50 and carried out an assessment of their effectiveness before expanding the programme so significantly. Whilst we welcome the Government's desire to invest resources in areas of educational under-achievement, we consider that the rapid expansion of the academy policy comes at the expense of rigorous evaluation . . .

The programme has been expanded without proper evidence to show that the current academies are working well. We asked Mr Clarke, the then Secretary of State, to describe the evidence base for the DfES academy programme and what evaluation of existing academy schools had taken place. He answered: 'Because we only have a very small number of academies at this moment, by definition you cannot have had a research programme to look at that relatively small number of academies before moving forward [. . .] I would say that a proper scientific assessment of the impact of academies could not meaningfully take place for two or three years at least, probably six or seven years of a school cohort going through, to assess what happened.'

The Secretary of State went on to say that 'the reason why academies are in a sense a diversion from the whole debate is that it is a very small number of schools out of all the secondary schools in Britain'. Although few in number, at an average cost of £25 million per school, academies represent a significant investment of resources.

The communities that will be served by academies are particularly vulnerable and have suffered from many years of inadequate education provision. We welcome the Government's desire to invest in the schools serving these communities. But the Government should ensure that the current programme of academies is thoroughly evaluated, both in respect of the performance of individual academies and the impact on neighbouring schools, before embarking on a major expansion of an untested model.

We fail to understand why the DfES is putting such substantial resources into academies when it has not produced the evidence on which to base the expansion of this programme . . .

As the Government continually repeats, the development of the academies programme is still in its early stages. As yet, the evidence for and against the initiative is primarily anecdotal. What evidence there is paints a mixed picture. Despite the paucity of evidence, the Government is enthusiastically pushing forward with the programme and with new academies. We caution against this approach and urge the DfES to monitor carefully the performance of academies and adjust its policies accordingly. In particular, the Department should consistently measure the proportion of pupils entitled to Free School Meals and the number of exclusions in academies.

The Government's reply to the committee was: 'We cannot wait five years for the study. These children only get one chance in life and we can't afford to wait that long before we make the radical break with the past, which academies represent.'

This is an appallingly dishonest answer. The Government likes to talk as though it can only make money available through this one mechanism. It likes us to think that, if you do not want academies, then you do not want public investment in our schools. But the Government could put the money, and the effort, into schools, without all the paraphernalia of sponsors, funding agreements and the rest. It could try something different. It chooses not to do so. By this choice, it gambles the future of all our children on a dreadfully flawed model.

11

Where Do We Go from Here?

The Government is spending an estimated £5 billion on the academies programme. And it would be churlish and wrong to say that the money has not done some good. Some good new schools have risen up over the ashes of rotting ones. That means a chance in life for thousands of children who would not otherwise have had one.

Lesley King of the Specialist Schools and Academies Trust says:

> The old schools were sometimes in a shocking state. In Walsall, the old school was knocked down and principals and staff went into temporary Portakabins for five terms. Ironically, the Portakabins were such an improvement on the old buildings that some pupils thought this was their new school.

Of course, the dreadful schools are not always the ones the academy programme is replacing, because academies are created wherever a sponsor is willing to create one. But where the interests of a sponsor coincide with the greatest need, some good has certainly been done.

It would also be churlish to condemn all the sponsors. Many of them (not all) are in it primarily because they see that education is the route out of poverty. And many of them (not all) have put in significant sums of money to try to make it an effective route.

These philanthropists are not to be despised. In the nine-teenth century, philanthropy was what provided such services as the poor got in terms of education, health care, and often even the most basic necessities of life. The rich looked at the desper-ate state of the poor in Victorian England, and, if they were not utterly without compassion, decided to use some of their wealth to help. That is what the best academy sponsors are doing. And if they choose the vanity of what Sir Cyril Taylor calls 'the monument principle' – creating the Harris Academy or the Jack Petchey Academy – then is that not just what nineteenth-century benefactors did? Is the work of, say, the Rowntree Foundation any less valuable for the fact that it is named after someone who made his fortune from sticky sweets?

But there were two problems with Victorian philanthropy. First, though there was quite a lot of it, there was never anything like enough. It could help a few individuals, but it could make little impact on the starvation and the slums; it could not stop thousands from dying for want of easily available medicine and care, nor thousands more living in starvation or near-starvation, and unable to get out of it for want of the most basic education and training. The problem was too big to be tackled by the voluntary contributions of a few rich men.

The second problem was spelled out most clearly in 1920 by Clement Attlee, who was to become Labour Prime Minister in 1945. A large chunk of his book *The Social Worker* was given over to explaining why the state needed to take over from the private philanthropist. If the rich wanted to help the poor, he wrote, then they should pay their taxes gladly. 'A right estab-lished by law, such as that to an old-age pension, is less galling than an allowance made by a rich man to a poor one, depending on his view of the recipient's character, and terminable at his caprice.' He quoted Robert Louis Stevenson, who called taxes 'the true charity, impartial and impersonal, cumbering none with obligation, helping all'.

Charity, Attlee wrote, 'is always apt to be accompanied by a certain complacency and condescension on the part of the benefactor; and by an expectation of gratitude from the recipient, which cuts at the root of all true friendliness'. The benefactor could also reasonably expect to decide how his money was spent.

For these reasons, in the early part of the twentieth century it became the view of the Labour Party – and broadly speaking remained so until 1997 – that the rich should aid the poor through the tax system, rather than by charitable gifts; and that education, health care, social security – all the elements of the 1945 Attlee settlement – should be paid for from taxation.

What city academies represent, therefore, is a return to the idea, condemned by Attlee, that the rich should contribute voluntarily, rather than through the tax system. But there is a new twist. The sponsor can get all the things a nineteenth-century philanthropist could get, and which Attlee grudged him: control of how the money is spent, a 'monument' to himself, the gratitude of the recipients. But unlike a nineteenth-century philanthropist, he does not have to pay the cost of the thing he is 'giving' – or even a substantial contribution towards the cost.

For in the city academy programme, the sponsors' money is practically irrelevant. The sponsor's £2 million is actually more like £1.2 million once the tax advantages are counted in. And if they all paid the full £2 million (most of them pay much less) then they would be putting in about £1 in every £25 that the programme will cost. Even that minimal contribution costs the Government millions of pounds every year to obtain, in staff time at the Specialist Schools and Academies Trust, development money for each academy, and splendid dinners at which Sir Cyril Taylor can bend the ears of wealthy people. To put it in commercial terms and business language: if you counted in everything it costs to leverage the money, the academies programme does not even wash its face.

What makes an academy is not private money, but public money. And academies have brought no educational benefits that could not have been obtained simply by putting in the amount of public money that has gone in. Even those benefits are confined to the children who attend academies. As Fiona Millar puts it: 'There are 3,500 secondary schools in this country, many of which have children with complex, disadvantaged home lives. How will putting £5 billion into 200 of them over the next five years help the pupils in all the rest?' Since she wrote this, the proposed number has gone up to 400, but the point remains valid. And a new system (more of this in a moment) means that sponsors' money will be even more irrelevant.

The reply from Lesley King, director of academy networks at the SSAT, is: 'It's not just academies that benefit from the money spent on them – they will influence the educational landscape for all schools.' But there is no evidence of this so far.

So we are left wondering what the Government's real intention is. It is investing a lot in academies – not just in money, but in political capital too. New Labour ministers may not care what the trade unions say – they may even think there are political advantages in being seen to be opposed by Labour's old friends in organized labour – but when all three teaching unions, which often do not agree with each other, combine to condemn something a Labour Government is doing, there is some sort of political price to be paid for continuing to do it.

Academies will 'benefit the few at the expense of the many' says the NUT. The NASUWT calls them 'privatization by stealth' and the ATL says they are 'not in the long-term interest of the provision of state education free to all'. Head teachers'

organizations, local government, support staff trade unions –
it's not easy to find anyone who thinks the academy model has
anything to offer.

At the SSAT, Lesley King points out that academies are what
is there. Reject them, and you may also be rejecting the money
that comes with them.

> I'm committed to the idea of something really systematic
> from the Government – a full-blooded attempt to do some-
> thing about giving all children a decent education. You seize
> on a programme like this which has significant good in it – I
> wasn't expecting perfection. I'm pragmatic enough not to say
> 'I won't touch it because it's not exactly what I want.'

She adds: 'The programme is part of a noble effort at decreasing
inequality' – and that, I fear, is where most commentators part
company with her.

Underlying what she says is the belief that, if academies are
rejected, the Government will punish education by taking the
money away. This may be true, but the Blair Government will
not be there for ever. Ministers are very defensive about the programme, and seem to be rushing to entrench it in the dying
days of Blair's premiership. Lord Adonis sometimes seems
honestly to believe that anyone who opposes it must also oppose
better schools for the poor. So what does the Government see
that everyone else misses?

I think it sees two big, long-term ideas for academies to fulfil
– and they are ideas which academies do stand a chance of
fulfilling. But there is a drawback. They are not ideas that a
Labour Government could own up to.

The new working class

British class distinction, we are frequently told, is on its way out. But it may be that it is simply adjusting to new circumstances, and academies are to play a key role in the new class distinction.

Education researcher Richard Hatcher of the University of Central England believes there is a new model of academy emerging. Its distinguishing marks will include a planned group of academies in one city, academies geared to local labour market needs, and academies sponsored by relevant local employers with the city council as co-sponsor.

We saw in Chapter 10 how perceived improvement in exam results from academies is often the result of a switch from academic GCSEs to vocational qualifications, or GNVQs. In academies with commercial sponsors in inner-city areas, there has been a flight away from GCSE and towards vocational qualifications. Richard Hatcher offers a typical example in 'Privatisation and Sponsorship':[1]

> In Bristol the academy focuses on vocational courses of study such as catering and hotel work. Parents are concerned that their children are not getting enough opportunity to follow academic courses, which is not how the academy was presented to them when it was first proposed.

Twenty-five of the existing 46 academies – more than half – have business and enterprise as their specialism, in some cases together with another specialism.

It looks as though the academies are destined to turn out the worker bees of industry. With the sponsor deciding both the specialism and the curriculum, they fulfil Sir Cyril Taylor's promise that they will be able to ensure that the next generation possesses the skills that industry requires.

But there is another sort of academy entirely, described at the end of Chapter 9. The best example of this is in the proposal for the United Learning Trust (ULT), already owners of several private fee-charging schools, to turn the private William Hulme's Grammar School in Manchester into an academy. This is a very long way from the idea of academies as a way of reviving poor inner-city schools. And there will certainly be no question of the William Hulme Academy moving its pupils away from academic GCSEs towards vocational GNVQs. Nor will it have business as its specialism; it will specialize in languages.

The local authority apparently expects it to have a thousand applications for 75 places. It will select 10 per cent of its pupils on aptitude for languages, and the rest on a banding system so that 90 per cent will be mixed ability. But when it comes to the sixth form, it will select, straightforwardly, on ability, and the sixth form will expand.

An interesting relationship is set to develop between this new academy and the existing Manchester Academy which opened in September 2003, is sponsored by ULT, and specializes, to no one's surprise, in business and enterprise. William Hulme head Stephen Patriarca and Manchester Academy head Kathy August have already discussed how it will work and Mr Patriarca explained it to me. Manchester Academy is stronger on vocational teaching, Hulme on academic teaching. When they get to the sixth form, pupils may change between the two: Hulme will send its vocational students to Manchester, Manchester will send its academic ones to Hulme.

Now, this, translated into a national system, is beginning to look horrifyingly familiar. After the 1944 Education Act, which provided for universal free education for everyone of school age, Britain created a three-tier system of grammar schools, technical schools and secondary modern schools. In practice, in most areas, the middle tier of technical schools never really took root. The system developed by the early 1950s into one in which each child sat the 11-plus examination; those who passed went to the grammar school, and those who failed went to the secondary modern. (We need not waste time over the political correctness of the day which demanded that we talked, not of passing and failing, but of being deemed suitable for a different kind of education.)

So in Manchester we are to have the academic former private school, with its elegant old buildings, its academic traditions (it used to be a direct grant school), selecting a small proportion of its intake at age 11 and becoming fully selective at 16, specializing in academic courses, for the education of the managing class; and the big, new, concrete school, good at vocational courses, specializing in 'business and enterprise' but not so hot on languages, or history, or literature, or pure science, turning out the new working class. It's exactly what horrified the then Labour Education Minister Ellen Wilkinson about the grammar school/secondary modern divide in 1948: giving what she called 'real education' to a small proportion, and educating the rest for their station in life, which is to keep the wheels of industry turning.

It ties in with a cynical (but realistic) reading of the Government's 14–19 strategy: that two routes are envisaged at age 14 – academic and vocational. It will be hard to mix the two because vocational studies are packaged into diplomas that take up most of the week. It will be in the interests of the 'secondary moderns' – places like the Manchester Academy – to persuade pupils and parents down the vocational route, which promises easier success for the pupils and a higher place in league tables for the school.

And what you get – as with secondary moderns – is the lower end of the ability range condemned to tedious training from the age of 14 onwards. But this time, unlike with the old secondary moderns, truanting will not be an alternative, since the Government is arming itself with formidable powers, including arbitrary detention for parents, to prevent it.

Who runs education?

The second big idea is about who runs education.

Tony Blair's first interest is religion. He is a man with strong, dominant, Christian beliefs, and his closest friends tend also to be Christians. Among academy sponsors, the one whom he finds personally and intellectually the most congenial is the Christian fundamentalist evangelist Sir Peter Vardy, whom he knighted.

In Chapter 5 we looked at Sir Peter's foundation, at its ideas and at the men who run it, and found that in 1995 Sir Peter's two closest educational advisers, John Burn and Nigel McQuoid, spelt out their long-term agenda in unmistakable terms: 'In Britain the Christian churches were active in the field of schooling long before the state took over . . . In retrospect it is a matter of regret that the churches so readily relinquished control of education to the state.' They want to see the state confine its activities in education to providing the money. How that money is spent should be taken out of the hands of the state, and given to the churches.

But what sort of British government will ever agree to such a thing? The Conservatives refused to do so, and the Conservative Education Secretary who created city technology colleges,

Kenneth Baker, is horrified that Labour's city academy programme involves handing so much power over to Christian
organizations. He refused to allow this to happen in his day.

The evangelists' literature makes it clear that they believe
they have, right now, the best chance they will ever have to
bring about a seismic shift of power in schools from the state to
the churches, while Tony Blair is Prime Minister. They seem
hardly able to believe their luck; they put it down to direct
divine intervention: 'It is only by God's sovereignty that current
legislation is couched in such advantageous terms in a country
where genuine committed Biblical Christian faith is undermined in so many areas.'[2] Personally, I'm sure that the very
favourable atmosphere for religious indoctrination in schools
today has less to do with God and far more to do with Tony
Blair. No doubt Messrs Burn and McQuoid would reply that
God has directed and inspired Mr Blair; and one gets the
impression that Mr Blair thinks so too.

It is a nightmare scenario for British education – that state
schools should be controlled by those who are committed to
indoctrinating our children with Christianity. The city academy
programme is the best chance they have ever had of making it a
reality.

It is not just the evangelicals. Catholics are thinking along
the same lines – and the Catholic Church is the one Tony Blair
is closest to, the one he will almost certainly formally join as
soon as he leaves Downing Street, and to which his wife is a
loyal, lifelong adherent.[3] Church control was what Michael
McGrath, education officer for the Catholic Church in
Scotland, meant when he told me: 'Catholic schools in Scotland
were transferred in 1918 to the state and the church was then
guaranteed certain rights.'

Catholics and evangelicals alike hope to ban those who do

not share their faith from teaching in their schools, whatever they find convenient to say to the contrary from time to time. 'All teachers in state Catholic schools in Scotland require the approval of the Catholic church in terms of religious belief and character. The [employment tribunal] judgement reaffirmed that this still applies, and to any teaching post', says Mr McGrath. 'If academies are to succeed,' says John Burn, 'they need to be led and staffed by people who are obedient to God's truth as revealed in the scriptures.'

As for the Church of England, here is the Rt Revd Peter Wheatley, Bishop of Edmonton, welcoming the announcement of academies in Haringey and Middlesbrough on 12 October 2000: 'The Churches were the original pioneers of school for inner-city communities and I am therefore especially delighted that the Diocese of London will also be pioneering a new City Academy in Haringey.' The Church of England does not have the militancy of the evangelicals and the Catholics, but it does sigh for the days when its writ ran in education.

Now, compare these aspirations with those of Professor Sir Michael Barber, one of the architects of Tony Blair's education policy: 'For most of the twentieth century the drive for educational progress came from the public sector. . . . Towards the end of the twentieth century, as frustration with existing systems grew, this legacy was challenged by a growing vibrant private sector.'[4]

Leave aside the politically correct adjectives (the private sector is always 'vibrant' in New Labourspeak) and what you are left with is a call for the state to relinquish control of education, from the man who, more than anyone except Mr Blair and Lord Adonis, is the thinker and strategist behind New Labour education policy. The new bosses can be churches or business people; or, as in the case of Sir Peter Vardy, both. The state – that is, you and I – provides the money, and the churches and such successful business people as wish to do so take the decisions. That is one of the reasons why the success of city academies matters so much to the Government that they are prepared to throw money at them at every opportunity, and to load the dice in their favour whenever possible. They are pioneers of an attempt to put the clock back to the days before the state involved itself in education.

The academy project's artificially prolonged life

The sheer arrogance of the academy scheme, by which sponsors and the Government decide what is best for local people and impose it on them, has caused ferocious local opposition in some areas. A few academy proposals have been defeated by people power.

We saw in Chapter 5 how the people of Conisbrough and Denaby saw off a Vardy academy. In Lambeth, south London, which already has one academy and another on the way, a third academy was planned on land occupied by Glenbrook Primary School and some council-owned sheltered housing. It was to be an all-age 3–19 academy, sponsored by ULT, and opening in 2008. But parents, teachers and governors all wanted Glenbrook to remain open, under local council control, and on its existing site. Their hand was strengthened by its excellent latest Ofsted report dating from November 2000, which called Glenbrook 'A very effective school, promoting pupils' personal development particularly well. Relationships within the school are very good. Children behave well and make very good progress.' The council was forced to withdraw the academy proposal, and Glenbrook remains open. An academy proposal in Wembley, north London, was seen off by trade unions and others, who pointed out the destabilizing effect it would have on neighbouring schools.

Such victories for what we can reasonably call people power are rare, but not unknown. Sometimes, as in Lambeth and in Conisbrough and Denaby, it is achieved by making it clear to councillors that they have to listen to the voters as well as the strident voices of governments and big corporations, if they want to keep their seats. Sometimes it is done by making the sponsor realize that the idea is very bad public relations. This is how Jasper Conran was persuaded to withdraw from sponsorship of an academy in Waltham Forest, north London, though the Government reacted by finding another sponsor, ULT, which is made of sterner stuff than Mr Conran, and, as a religious organization, has a proselytizing motive which Mr Conran lacked.

But these are occasional and isolated victories. The Newcastle and Islington pattern is more common: where the people indicate that they do not want city academies by electing a council which opposes them, only to find that the councillors are forced either to go along the academy route, or watch a vengeful government starve their schools of cash and watch them rot.

In any case, the original academies model is sinking under its own weight, and being quietly replaced with something very different. First to go was the idea that they replaced failing schools. Then the name 'city academy' was, ever so quietly, dropped; the preferred term now is 'academy', to take account of the fact that they are no longer seen as a way of reviving inner-city schools.

Next to go was the idea that they were aimed squarely at the poorest families. The parents who pay £8,148 a year to send their children to William Hulme School in Manchester may not be rich, but they are self-evidently not among the poorest either. This was, in the end, the only way Lord Adonis could get fee-charging schools involved. The idea that the poshest public schools were going to put up money to recreate struggling inner-city schools – 'the Eton Academy, the Winchester Academy' of David Miliband's dream – has come to almost nothing.

As commercial sponsors started to dry up, the Government started to drag in organizations like the Royal Society for the Arts (RSA). A letter to RSA members in October 2006 about its proposed new academy in Tipton, in the West Midlands, is signed by Sir Mike Tomlinson, former Ofsted chief; but from its breathless wording it clearly comes out of the New Labour school of spin: 'I can't say how excited I am . . .' 'Share our vision . . .' 'Transforming it to the RSA Academy'. (New Labour never changes things, it always transforms them.)

The letter asks its Fellows to put in £50 each to help sponsor a city academy. This is a long, long way from the idea of corporate sponsors. This is ordinary people being asked to put up money for state education. How far are we from having charity collectors standing on street corners rattling tins in order to raise money for schools?

Academies are supposed to take schools away from the dead hand of local authorities and hand them to dynamic private sponsors (except, as we have seen, on the Isle of Sheppey in Kent, where the academy sponsor is none other than the local authority).

But commercial sponsors are getting very hard to find. The cost is proving too great, and the association with New Labour sleaze is proving deadly. The big household name companies never came in, and business moguls like Roger de Haan and Lord Harris are coming to the end of the money they are prepared to commit. The churches, and associated organizations like the United Learning Trust, would like to fill the gap, but they are competing for a dwindling pool of commercial sponsors with the

SSAT fundraisers Lord Levy and Sir Cyril Taylor. ULT, the biggest and most successful of all of them, is hampered by having to avoid treading on the toes of Government fundraisers. It is no use ULT trying to touch a multi-millionaire for money at the same time as Lord Levy is trying to touch the same multi-millionaire.

Churches will not use their own money: with their dwindling congregations, they have to watch their pennies.

So there is a new dispensation, announced in the dying days of 2006, which gets rid of the requirement for sponsors to provide a £2 million capital contribution. From now on, academies will be built entirely with public money. Sponsors will only be expected to make annual revenue contributions to the new Academy Trusts. The new rules seek an initial contribution of £500,000, with additional funds paid over a five-year period to total £2 million (or £1.5 million where a sponsor is involved in sponsoring a programme of four or more academies.)

It makes entry much easier for sponsors. It increases their already almost total power over what the academies do from year to year. It strips away the last pretence that academies are to get the same funding as other state schools. This pretence relied on the fact that, while they had a great deal more capital funding, they had the same amount of recurrent funding. Now even this will no longer be true.

The new dispensation was the nearest politicians ever get to saying: this idea was a dud. It was therefore sneaked out in the practised New Labour way. Its spin doctors know that there are more places in which to bury bad news than under the rubble of the World Trade Center. The press release announcing the change was headlined 'Parent power and new independent report give fresh backing to academies'. It wittered for several paragraphs about how academies must be wonderful because parents couldn't get their children into some of them (choosing the ones it cited extremely carefully), and quoted all the positive bits and none of the negative ones from the PricewaterhouseCoopers report, which it chose to describe as independent. Then it had Education Secretary Alan Johnson blathering on for ever about how wonderful everything was. And then, in the ninth paragraph, it said: 'Also announced today is a new sponsorship model.' It disposed of the bad news in just three convoluted and almost incomprehensible sentences. By that time, most journalists had stopped reading and filed it under 'Boring government puffery'. Then it covered its tracks, with a further mind-numbing 17 paragraphs of straight marketingspeak.

But all the spin in the world will not rescue the project, which, at least in its original form, is dying. We have to work out what we want to replace it. Here's my stab at it.

Finding a better way

Defending the academy programme, Lesley King of the SSAT said to me: 'Students can think they are in second-class schools for second-class children.' One of the charges against academies is that they make this more likely. But any alternative to the academies project has to start by facing the fact that the problem which academies were supposed to confront is real.

There are many schools, seriously under-resourced and sometimes badly run, which are buckling under the strain, and the life chances of their pupils are seriously diminished. The Government, to its credit, has shown willingness to put money into this problem. Businesses and churches have shown much less willingness to do so, and their contribution might be much better made – as Clement Attlee wanted – by paying their taxes willingly and joyfully, knowing that these were achieving the objective.

The Thatcher Government began, and the Blair Government continued, the process of disempowering local government. The Blair Government has now effectively removed any real role for elected local politicians in education. In 2005 a secret crib for spin doctors to the Education White Paper showed that, in the long term, the policy will effectively abolish the cornerstone of the 1944 Education Act: the duty on local authorities to find a school place for all school-age children in their areas.

The crib, marked 'Restricted – policy', is designed to give answers to all the charges levelled against the White Paper. It offers a list of common criticisms, complete with a 'rebuttal' for each one.

One of the common criticisms listed is: 'There is no role for local authorities in the new system.' To this, spin doctors are instructed to answer: 'Not at all. We see the local authority as the champion of parents and pupils, commissioning rather than providing education.' There follows a page full of the usual feelgood words – choice, diversity, champion, choice, innovation, partnership, diversity, especially choice – all tumbling over each other like excited children. But later in the document, a brief note says that the Government is abolishing the 'notion' of a local education authority (LEA). The term 'Local Education Authority' is to be removed from the statute book. Local authorities are to lose their specialist arm which deals with education.

Schools are 'to become self-governing independent schools, with autonomy over staffing, premises and admissions that are in the school's best interests'. If schools have autonomy over admissions, then local authorities cannot direct them to take a pupil. And if there is no school which can be directed to take a pupil, the local authority cannot exercise its statutory duty to find a place for all children.

In city academies, the sponsor takes on the powers which were once exercised by the local authority. But it is no part of a sponsor's duty to ensure that every school-age child in the area gets an education. As we have seen, city academies have been known to do the opposite. They sometimes offload their problem pupils for the local authority to look after. And increasingly, local authorities cannot do so.

Now there is to be no LEA, and no power to instruct a school. A DfES spokesman told me: 'It will still be the duty of a local authority to make sure each child has a place. But if the local authority is unable to help, it will end up going to the Secretary of State.' It is not at all clear what the Secretary of State can do about it. It is hard to see this sort of centralized command-and-control working well, or even working at all.

Academies strip the last shreds of democracy out of our school system. Once, you could elect councillors who took decisions about education, and, if you were a parent, elect parent governors who took decisions about your school. All those decisions are now firmly in the hands of the sponsor.

The SSAT tends rather to sneer at the old democratic principle, asking pointedly if parents felt they were in charge. The answer, of course, is no. Democracy was, to put it kindly, imperfect. But how far does the individual feel in charge of, say, Government foreign policy? Hardly at all, I suspect; but that is not an argument for taking the vote away from us. Winston Churchill's maxim still stands: democracy is the worst method of government, except for all the others. Can we improve democracy, instead of abolishing it?

Weak as it may be on parents' rights, the spinners' crib is strong on punishing them. It proposes 'extending parenting contracts and orders, so that schools . . . can use them to force parents to take responsibility for their children's bad behaviour in schools'. Parents will also be required to take responsibility for excluded pupils in the first five days of a suspension, by ensuring that they are 'properly supervised doing schoolwork at home', with fines for parents if 'pupils are found unsupervised during school hours'. In the case of Jack, whose case I discussed in Chapter 5, how would this work? His mother is a single parent who needs to go out to work every day to feed her family, and she pleaded with the King's Academy in Middlesbrough to take him back. Jack was not out of school for five days, but for five months, since his local authority's powers are already so weak, and its resources so small, that they often cannot find a place.

Schools minister Jim Knight told the New Local Government Network in October 2006: 'Local authorities will be the champions for children, the fighters for families in their areas. But that means taking a step back from schools in order to stand up for families.' This is rubbish. Anyone can 'stand up for families'. If a council is to do anything concrete for them, it has to have the power to do it.

Replacing LEAs with a national 'family' of schools, such as the large and growing family run by the United Learning Trust, does not do the job. First, it does not fulfil that requirement of the 1944 Act which lies at the heart of universal state education – it does nothing to ensure that every child of school age gets a school place. And second, it does not provide for local people to have a say in the education on offer in their area. In fact, it takes all power away from the people the schools are designed to serve. Third, as we have seen, it is not even efficient. ULT's failure to get its school built in time in Paddington (see Chapter 10) shows that there is no private sector gold dust which can save us from the failures of the public sector

Education has been partly privatized, and partly nationalized. Power which was once exercised by locally elected politicians is now exercised either by big corporations and churches, or by huge national bureaucracies, like the Learning and Skills Council, which is now responsible for 16–19 (and increasingly 14–19) education.

But the idea that education should be simply returned to local government would bring a universal, and justified, groan. Local government is widely seen as bureaucratic and inefficient, and there is no doubt that today a lot of it is, especially since there is no real power there. No one who wants to change the world, and who has a realistic understanding of where power lies, stands for their local council today, and the quality of local councillors and officials has been steadily declining for two decades. As their powers decline, so do the numbers of people who bother to turn out to vote in local elections. We do not want schools enmeshed in layers of local government bureaucracy.

Not all LEAs were bad. Some were. But some have been among the brightest, most innovative organizations in education, leading and inspiring the schools in their area. The Inner London Education Authority, abolished by the Thatcher Government, did some fine things and is remembered with respect by those who worked under it. More recently, Birmingham, under the leadership of Tim Brighouse, was widely recognized, not least by the head teachers it employed, as having improved Birmingham's schools enormously, and given them a new confidence and self-respect.

What perhaps distinguishes these two is that they were not just another council committee: they were strong entities in their own right.

There are far too many LEAs for them to run education – we have 150 of them, and many are very small indeed – and they are not sufficiently distinguishable from the other things a local authority is nominally in charge of.

Could we have strong local organizations, democratically accountable, which can use money efficiently, ensure that local parents are given the schools they believe their children should have, and have the resources to ensure that every child, however poor and however badly behaved, gets an education that brings out the best in them? Could we have such organizations without having them weighed down by local government bureaucracy?

All the evidence we have suggests that, if there is one thing people care about and have views about, it is the education of their children. They are willing to put time, effort and thought into managing it – witness the thousands of unpaid school governors (though these are being sidelined in city academies, where the sponsor will always have an inbuilt majority on the governing body).

If people are no longer putting themselves up to be local councillors, and no longer bothering to vote in council elections, it is largely because they do not seem to make a difference. But there would be many committed, knowledgeable people who would want to be on directly elected bodies with real power – let us for the moment call them Local Education Councils (LECs) – whose job it was to spend the education budget wisely and efficiently, to run the local school system, to ensure that every local school was successful and well run, and allowed children to succeed, and which had real power to achieve this.

Each one would need to have a sufficiently large area to take real strategic decisions. There are 150 LEAs, which is far too many, and a lot of them, especially in the London boroughs, are too small. As to the inevitable charge that it would be another layer of expensive bureaucracy, it would be a lot cheaper and less bureaucratic than the multiple layers we have now. It would enable us to lose all of these: the toothless LEAs, now supposed to be 'the champion of parents' but with no properly defined duties or powers; the Specialist Schools and Academies Trust, a bloated and pointless national quango which finds and services sponsors; the millions that go to consultants in advance of every academy; and the hugely expensive Government fundraising operation.

It would not preclude sponsors, either. Why should not the LECs be able to seek sponsorship if they wish to do so, and if they can get it? The difference, though, is that the sponsor's money would not buy control. The LECs would run the schools, not the sponsors, and they would have the legitimacy of being elected specifically to do so.

And whether or not a big business chose to sponsor a school, it would be paying for education through its taxes, which means that every company would be paying, not just those which choose to sponsor a school. This is a far fairer way of distributing the burden. Every company needs a trained and educated workforce; why should only those who volunteer to do so pay for it?

What about the existing city academies? They would need to be looked at one by one. Each funding agreement contains conditions upon which the academy can be returned to the public sector, and each is different. Some would fit well into the new structure – it is hard to see, say, the academy on the Isle of Sheppey proving a great problem, since the main sponsor is the local authority. It may be that in some cases there is a restrictive legally binding funding agreement and an obdurate commercial or religious sponsor, and it would remain, anachronistically, outside the local family of schools.

The idea would help to revive local democracy, by giving people something to vote for which matters and which they care about. It would provide real power for parents, which is a lot better than the sham power of being able to 'choose' schools. It would make those who took decisions about schools genuinely accountable.

It would mean a reversal of nearly 30 years of education policy, during which the thrust has been to make education policy more 'top down' – the pinnacle of which is the city academy policy. Power, progressively taken away from the people over the last 30 years, would return to the people.

Set the people free, and let them choose. You might be surprised at how well they use their freedom.

Notes

1.   *Journal of Education Policy*, 2006.
2.   *Christianity and the School Curriculum*, Christian Institute, 1995.
3.   Francis Beckett and David Hencke, *The Survivor: Tony Blair in Peace and War*, Aurum, 2005.
4.   Quoted in Hatcher: 'Privatisation and Sponsorship', *Journal of Education Policy*, 2006.

Appendix 1

Academies Open as at September 2006

There are currently 46 academies open. The first three academies opened in September 2002 and nine in September 2003. Five academies opened in September 2004, ten in September 2005 and a further 19 opened in September 2006. Listed here are key facts for each institution.

The Business Academy, Bexley

School
Co-educational for 11–19-year-olds

Specialism
Business and enterprise

Local authority
Bexley

Sponsor
Sir David Garrard, Chairman of the Garrard Education Trust

Principal
Duncan Spalding

Open
September 2002 – new building completed September 2003. Opened as an All-Age Academy, September 2004.

Size
The school roll is currently 1,820, incuding a sixth form of 350

History
Replaced Thamesmead Community College

Website
http://www.thebusinessacademy.org

Greig City Academy, Harringey

School
Co-educational for 11–18-year-olds

Specialism
ICT

Local authority
Haringey

Sponsor
The Greig Trust with the Diocese of London

Principal
Paul Sutton

Open
September 2002

Size
School roll is currently
1,250, including a sixth form of 175

History
Replaced St David and St Katherine
Church of England High Schools

Website
http://www.greigcityacademy.co.uk

**Unity City Academy,
East Middlesbrough**

School
Co-educational for 11–16-year-olds

Specialism
ICT

Local authority
East Middlesbrough

Sponsor
Amey plc

Principal
Bob Dore

Open
September 2002. Moved into new
buildings in September 2004

Size
Currently 1,200 on roll

History
Replaced Keldholme and
Langbaurgh Schools

Website
http://www/unityacademy.org

Capital City Academy, Brent

School
Co-educational for 11–18-year-olds

Specialism
Sports

Local authority
Brent

Sponsor
Sir Frank Lowe

Principal
Philip O'Hear

Open
September 2003 in a new building

Size
Currently has 1,200 pupils on roll
with a sixth form of 250.

History
Replaced Willesden High School

Website
http://www.capitalcityacademy.org

The City Academy, Bristol

School
Co-educational for 11–18-year-olds

Specialism
Sports

Local authority
Bristol

Sponsor
John Laycock and the University of the West of England

Principal
Ray Priest

Open
September 2003. New building completed September 2005

Size
Currently 1,250 on roll, including sixth form of 250

History
Replaced St George Community College

Website
http://www.cityacademybristol.co.uk

The West London Academy, Ealing

School
Co-educational for 11–18-year-olds

Specialism
Sports and enterprise

Local authority
Ealing

Sponsor
Alec Reed, Chairman of Reed Executive plc

Principal
Hillary Macaulay

Open
September 2003

Size
Currently 1,150 on roll including sixth form of 250

History
Replaced Compton Sports College

Website
http://www.westlondonacademy.co.uk

Manchester Academy, Manchester

School
Co-educational for 11–19-year-olds

Specialism
Business enterprise and art

Local authority
Manchester

Sponsor
United Learning Trust and Manchester Science Park

Principal
Kathy August

Open
September 2003. Moved to new building January 2005

Size
Currently 1,150 on roll including sixth form of 250

History
Replaced Ducie High School,
Moss Side

Website
http://www.manchester-academy.org

King's Academy, Middlesbrough

School
Co-educational for 11–18-year-olds

Specialism
Business and enterprise

Local authority
Middlesbrough

Sponsor
Emmanuel Schools Foundation

Principal
Chris Drew

Open
September 2003 in new building

Size
Currently 1,250 on roll, including
sixth form of 250

History
Replaced Brackenhoe Comprehensive
and Coulby Newham Schools

**Djanogly City Academy,
Nottingham**

School
Co-educational for 11–19-year-olds

Specialism
ICT

Local authority
Nottingham

Sponsor
Sir Harry Djanogly

Principal
Mike Butler

Open
August 2003

Size
Currently 1,628 on roll including
sixth form of 147

History
Replaced Djanogly CTC and Forest
School

**City of London Academy
(Southwark)**

School
Co-educational for 11–19-year-olds

Specialism
Business and enterprise, sports

Local authority
Southwark

Sponsor
Corporation of London

Principal
Martyn Coles

Open
September 2003 in new building

Size
Currently has 1,200 on roll,
including sixth form of 300

History
New school

Website
http://www.thecityoflondonacademy.
co.uk

_____

**The Academy at Peckham,
Southwark**

School
Co-educational for 11–19-year-olds

Specialism
Business and performing arts

Local authority
Southwark

Sponsor
Lord Harris of Peckham

Principal
Peter Crook

Open
September 2003

Size
Currently 1,450 on roll, including
sixth form of 250

History
Replaced Warwick Park School

Website
http://www.peckhamacademy.
southwark.sch.uk

_____

Walsall City Academy

School
Co-educational for 11–18-year-olds

Specialism
Technology

Local authority
Walsall

Sponsor
Thomas Telford Online and the
Mercers' Company

Principal
Jean Hickman

Open
September 2003

Size
Currently 1,200 pupils on roll,
including sixth form of 300

History
Replaced TP Riley School

Website
http://www.walsallacademy.com

The London Academy, Barnet

School
Co-educational for 11–19-year-olds,
with a speech and language unit

Specialism
Business and enterprise, technology

Local authority
Barnet

Sponsor
Peter Shalson, Chairman SGI Ltd

Principal
Phil Herne

Open
September 2004, and will have moved
to new building September 2006

Size
Currently 1,238 on roll, including
sixth form of 153

Website
http://www.londonacademy.org.uk

**Mossbourne Community Academy,
Hackney**

School
Co-educational for 11–19-year-olds

Specialism
Technology

Local authority
Hackney

Sponsor
Sir Clive Bourne, Life President of
Seabourne Group plc

Principal
Sir Michael Wilshaw

Open
September 2004

Size
Currently 900 on roll

History
New school

Website
http://www.mossbourne.hackney.
sch.uk

Stockley Academy, Hillingdon

School
Co-educational for 11–18-year-olds

Specialism
Science and technology

Local authority
Hillingdon

Sponsor
Barry Townsley, of Insinger
Townsley Stockbrokers and others

Principal
Fred Groom

Open
September 2004. Moved to new
buildings September 2005

Size
1,150 currently on roll. 250 in sixth form

History
Replaced Evelyns Community School

Website
http://www.stockleyacademy.com

Lambeth Academy, Lambeth

School
Co-educational for 11–18-year-olds

Specialism
Business and enterprise, languages

Local authority
Lambeth

Principal
Stephen Potter

Open
September 2004

Size
Currently 900 on roll

History
New school

Website
http://www.lambeth-academy.org

Northampton Academy, Northampton

School
Co-educational for 11–18-year-olds

Specialism
Sports, business and enterprise

Local authority
Northampton

Sponsor
United Learning Trust

Principal
Rt Revd Peter Hullah

Open
September 2004 and will move to new building September 2006

Size
Currently 1,420 on roll, including sixth form of 220

History
Replaced Lings Upper School

Trinity Academy, Doncaster

School
Co-educational for 11–18-year-olds

Specialism
Business and enterprise

Local authority
Doncaster

Sponsor
Emmanuel Schools Foundation

Principal
I. Brew

Open
September 2005

Size
1,470 currently on roll, including
sixth form of 350

History
Replaced Thorne Grammar School

St Paul's Academy, Greenwich

School
Co-educational for 11–16-year-olds

Specialism
Sports and enterprise

Local authority
Greenwich

Sponsor
The Roman Catholic Diocese of
Southwark

Principal
P. Winston

Open
September 2005 in current
building. New building will be
completed in 2007

Size
Currently 1,200 pupils on roll

History
Replaced St Paul's Roman Catholic
Voluntary Aided School

Salford City Academy, Salford

School
Co-educational for 11–16-year-olds

Specialism
Business and enterprise, sports

Local authority
Salford

Principal
Elizabeth Haddock

Open
September 2005. Moved to new
building September 2006

Size
Currently 950 on roll

History
Replaced Canon Williamson
Church of England School

Website
http://www.salfordcity-
academy.org.uk

(Note: The DfES lists no sponsor
for this academy but it is in fact the
United Learning Trust.)

Marlowe Academy, Kent

School
Co-educational for 11–18-year-olds

Specialism
Business and performing arts

Local authority
Kent

Sponsor
Roger de Haan and Kent County
Council

Principal
Ian Johnson

Open
September 2005

History
Replaced Ramsgate School

**The Harefield Academy,
Hillingdon**

School
Co-educational for 11–18-year-olds

Specialism
Sports

Local authority
Hillingdon

Sponsor
David Meller

Principal
Lynn Gadd

Open
September 2005

Size
Currently 1,000 on roll, including
sixth form of 250

History
Replaced John Penrose School

**Haberdashers' Aske's Knights
Academy, Lewisham**

School
Co-educational for 11–18-year-olds

Specialism
Sports

Local authority
Lewisham

Sponsor
Haberdashers' Company

Principal
Yvonne McCallum

Open
September 2005

Size
Currently 1,050 on roll

History
Replaced Malory School

Website
http://www.hahc.org.uk

Haberdashers' Aske's Hatcham College Academy, Lewisham

School
Co-educational for 11–18-year-olds

Specialism
ICT and music

Local authority
Lewisham

Sponsor
Haberdashers' Company

Principal
Michelle Adamson

Open
September 2005

Size
Currently 1,340 on roll, including sixth form of 300

History
Haberdashers' Aske's Hatcham College Academy was converted from Haberdashers' Aske's City Technology College (CTC)

Website
http://www.hahc.org.uk

———————

Dixons City Academy, Bradford

School
Co-educational for 11–16-year-olds

Specialism
Performing arts and product design

Local authority
Bradford

Sponsor
Dixons CTC

Principal
Nick Weller

Open
September 2005

Size
Currently 1,060 on roll, including sixth form of 260

History
Replaced Dixons City Technology College

———————

Academy of St Francis Assisi, Liverpool

School
Co-educational for 11–16-year-olds

Specialism
The environment

Local authority
Liverpool

Sponsor
Diocese of Liverpool and the Roman Catholic Archdiocese of Liverpool

Principal
J. Burke

Open
September 2005

Size
Currently 900 on roll

History
Replaced Our Lady's Catholic High
School

**Macmillan Academy,
West Middlesbrough**

School
Co-educational for 11–18-year-olds

Specialism
Science, PE and outdoor education

Local authority
Middlesbrough

Sponsor
Macmillan CTC

Principal
K. Fraser

Open
September 2005

Size
Currently 1,435 on roll, including
sixth form of 335

History
Macmillan City Technology College
was converted to become
Macmillan Academy. The academy
is a DfES designated Training
School for Teachers and is the only
school in the country to be a
training centre for National College
for School Leadership (NCSL)
Courses.

**Westminster Academy,
Westminster**

School
Co-educational for 11–18-year-olds

Specialism
International business and
enterprise

Local authority
Westminister

Sponsor
Exilarch's Foundation

Principal
Alison Banks

Open
September 2006

Size
Currently 1,175 on roll

History
Replaced North Westminister
Community School

The Petchey Academy, Hackney

School
Co-educational for 11–18-year-olds

Specialism
Health care and medical sciences

Local authority
Hackney

Sponsor
Jack Petchey Foundation

Open
September 2006

Size
Currently 181 on roll

History
New school

website:
http://www.petcheyacademy.org.uk

_____

The John Madejski Academy, Reading

School
Co-educational for 11–18-year-olds

Specialism
Sports

Local authority
Reading

Principal
Catherine Shaw

Open
September 2006

Size
Currently 1,100 on roll

History
Replaced Thamesbridge
Community College

_____

Paddington Academy, Westminster

School
Co-educational for 11–18-year-olds

Specialism
Media and the performing arts with
business and enterprise

Local authority
Westminster

Sponsor
United Learning Trust

Principal
Barbi Goulding

Open
September 2006

Size
Currently 1,175 on roll

History
Replaced North Westminster
Community School

David Young Community Academy, Leeds

School
Co-educational for 11–18-year-olds

Specialism
Design and the built environment

Local authority
Leeds

Sponsor
Church of England

Principal
Ros McMullen

Open
September 2006

Size
Currently 1,170 on roll

History
Replaced Agnes Stewart and Braim Wood Schools

Barnsley Academy, Barnsley

School
Co-educational for 11–18-year-olds

Specialism
Science with business and enterprise

Local authority
Barnsley

Sponsor
United Learning Trust

Open
September 2006

Size
Currently 1,150 on roll

History
Replaced Elmhirst School

Walthamstow Academy, Waltham Forest

School
Co-educational for 11–18-year-olds

Specialism
Business and enterprise, science and maths

Local authority
Waltham Forest

Sponsor
United Learning Trust

Principal
Fiona Cordeaux

Open
September 2006

Size
Currently 1,150 on roll

History
Replaced McEntee School

**Sheffield Springs Academy,
Sheffield**

School
Co-educational for 11–18-year-olds

Specialism
Performing arts and technology

Local authority
Sheffield

Sponsor
United Learning Trust

Principal
Gordon Inglis

Open
September 2006

Size
Currently 1,300 on roll

History
Replaced Myrtle Springs School

Sheffield Park Academy, Sheffield

School
Co-educational for 11–18-year-olds

Specialism
Business and enterprise

Local authority
Sheffield

Sponsor
United Learning Trust

Principal
Andy Gardiner

Open
September 2006

Size
Currently 1,300 on roll

History
Replaced Waltheof School

The Harris Academy, Bermondsey

School
11–18 years – girls

Specialism
Enterprise

Local authority
Bermondsey

Principal
Catherine Loxton

Open
September 2006

Size
Currently 1,150 on roll

History
Replaced Alwin Girls' School

Website
http://www.hgaed.org.yl

Harris Academy, Merton

School
Co-educational for 11–18-year-olds

Specialism
Sports and enterprise

Local authority
Merton

Sponsor
Lord Harris of Peckham

Principal
Andy Halpin

Open
September 2006

Size
Currenty 1,200 on roll

History
Replaced Tamworth Manor High
School

**Harris Girls Academy,
East Dulwich**

School
11–18 years – girls

Specialism
Sports, PE and health

Local authority
Southwark

Sponsor
Lord Harris of Peckham

Principal
Lesley Day

Open
September 2006

Size
Currently 950 on roll

History
Replaced Waverley Girls School

Landau Forte College, Derby

School
Co-educational for 11–18-year-olds

Specialism
Technology and business enterprise

Local authority
Derby

Sponsor
Landau Foundation

Open
September 2006

Size
Currently 1,120 on roll

History
Replaced Landau Forte City
Technology College

Sandwell Academy, Sandwell

School
Co-educational for 11–18-year-olds

Specialism
Business and enterprise, sports

Local authority
Sandwell

Sponsors
Mercers Company, Thomas Telford
Online, HSBC
West Bromwich Albion FC, Tarmac
Group

Principal
Dave Berry

Open
September 2006

Size
Currently 1,200 on roll

History
New school

———————

Grace Academy, Solihull

School
Co-educational for 11–18-year-olds

Specialism
Business and enterprise

Local authority
Solihull

Sponsor
Bob Edmiston

Principal
David Wootton

Open
September 2006

Size
Currently 1,350 on roll

History
Replaced Whitesmore School

———————

**St Mark's Church of England
Academy, Merton**

School
Co-educational for 11–18-year-olds

Specialism
Science and enterprise

Local authority
Merton

Sponsor
Southwark Diocese

Principal
Louise Fox

Open
September 2006

Size
Currently 1,200 on roll

History
Replaced Mitcham Vale School

Website
http://www.stmarksacademy.com

Gateway Academy, Thurrock

School
Co-educational for 11–18-year-olds

Local authority
Thurrock

Sponsor
Ormiston Trust

Principal
Margaret Wilson

Open
September 2006

History
Replaced Gateway Community
College

**North Liverpool Academy,
Liverpool**

School
Co-educational for 11–18-year-olds

Specialism
Business and enterprise

Local authority
Liverpool

Sponsor
Liverpool University and Granada
Learning

Principal
Kay Askew

Open
September 2006

Size
Currently 1,750 on roll

History
Replaced Anfield and Breckfield
Schools

Information from DfES's standards
website, October 2006:
http://www.standards.dfes.gov.uk/
academies/projects/openacademies/
?version=1

Funding Agreements can be found
on the DfES's Freedom of
Information site at:
http://www.dfes.gov.uk/foischeme/
by putting the word 'academies' in
the search box.

Appendix 2

Timeline

15 March 2000
Education Secretary David Blunkett announces the introduction of city academies in a speech to the Social Market Foundation.

23 March 2000
In budget debate, Blunkett announces £60 million capital to support academies.

27 July 2000
Learning and Skill Act receives royal assent. S130–3 and Schedule 8 provide for city academies.

15 September 2000
First three academies announced to start in September 2002. They were in:

Brent: to replace Willesden High School, and to be sponsored by Frank Lowe, Chairman of Lowe Group and Octagon Sports Marketing, who gave £1.5 million for a sports academy.
Lambeth: to be sponsored by CfBT (Centre for British Teachers) and to be a technology academy. No figures given as to amount of sponsorship. In the event CfBT said it had no money for sponsorship.
Liverpool: sponsored by Church of England and local businesses including Marconi and BT and to be a technology academy. No figures given as to amount of sponsorship.

12 October 2000
Two more academies announced in:

Haringey: to be sponsored by the Church of England and the Greig Trust. £600,000 announced as sponsorship for the £3 million refurbishment. To be a technology academy and to replace St David and St Katharine High School.
East Middlesbrough: city academy sponsored by up to £2 million and support in kind from Amey plc'. To be a technology academy.

18 December 2000
Sixth academy announced in Hillingdon with a technology specialism. Promised state-of-art computer facilities linked to high-tech businesses and Brunel University. To replace Evelyns Community School. Sponsor is Barry Townsley with £1.5 million of private funding. He is chair of stockbrokers Insinger Townsley. Additional sponsors include CISCO (civil service catering organization), Brunel University, HASBRO (toy manufacturer), Jarvis plc and BAA.

21 March 2001
First business and enterprise academies announced:

Southwark: sponsor to be Corporation of London with £2 million. Called City of London Academy.
Bexley: sponsor to be David Garrard (chair of Minerva plc) with £2 million. To replace Thamesmead Community College.
Walsall: with a technology specialism. Sponsored by Thomas Telford Online (offshoot of Thomas Telford School, a city technology college) and the Mercers' Company with £2 million. Will replace TP Riley School.

10 July 2001
Three new academies announced in:

Barnet: business and enterprise and IT academy. Sponsor Peter Shalson, Chairman of SGI Ltd. To replace Edgware School. £1.5 million sponsorship.
Manchester: science academy. Sponsor Manchester Science Park Ltd. Replaces Ducie High School. Sponsorship of only £225,000 announced.
South Middlesbrough: sponsor Emmanuel Schools Foundation (Sir Peter Vardy). Business and finance specialism. To replace Brachenhoe and Coulby Newham Schools. £2 million sponsorship.

4 December 2001
Two academies announced:

Bristol: replaces St George Community College. Sport specialism. Sponsor is a consortium led by Bristol City Football Club and University of the West of England. £2 million pledged.
Nottingham: combines Djanogly CTC (named after sponsor Sir Harry) and The Forest Community School. ICT specialism.

28 January 2002
Seventeenth academy announced in north Liverpool to replace Breckfield and Anfield Schools. Sponsor is property developer-turned-philanthropist Cyril Dennis who is contributing £2 million. Academy to be designed by Richard Rogers.

Education Act 2002
Allows for city academies in rural areas and for all-age primary up to sixth-form academies. Also allows CTCs to become academies. Bexley (opened in September 2002) trying to establish itself as a 4–18 academy.

8 October 2003
Minister of State for School Standards David Miliband calls for private schools with endowed foundations to put their intellectual resources, practical experience and financial muscle at the disposal of academies. Hints this will help protect their charitable status.

12 May 2003
DfES announces 30 city academies in London by 2008, as well as two new academies sponsored by Oasis, a Christian charity, and North London Collegiate School.

2003
Government commissioned a report by PricewaterhouseCoopers on academies, but suppresses it when it is delivered. It says academies could lead to a two-tier system based on social class.

May 2006
Edinburgh University study into results of first 11 academies shows they have failed to improve results.

June 2006
There are 27 city academies open and 49 in development. Target is 200 open or in pipeline by 2010, 60 of them in London.

July 2006
Legal challenges by parents to proposed academies in Merton, Islington and the Isle of Sheppey, Kent.

October 2006

Forty-six academies open. Government announces, in tenth paragraph of a press release, that academies will in future be built entirely with public money. Sponsors will only be expected to make annual revenue contributions to the new Academy Trusts. The new rules seek an initial contribution of £500,000 with additional funds paid over a five-year period to total £2 million (or £1.5 million where a sponsor is involved in sponsoring a programme of four or more academies).

Appendix 3

Academies that Are in Development

These are academy projects that are either in the implementation stage (having signed a funding agreement) or are in the feasibility stage (having submitted a formal expression of interest and undergoing investigation and consultation).

They are shown here in alphabetical order with local authorities.

Archbishop Michael Ramsey Church of England
Southwark

Bacon's – a Church of England Sponsored Academy
Southwark

Barnfield West and Central Academy
Luton

Barnfield and South and East Central Academy
Luton

(Academy name to be confirmed)
Barnet

The Belvedere Academy
Liverpool

Blackburn with Darwen
Blackburn with Darwen

Blyth Academy
Northumberland

Bradford Academy
Bradford

Bulwell (Enterprise) Business Academy
Nottingham

The Brit School
Croydon

The Bridge Academy
Hackney

Castleview Academy
Sunderland

The Chelsea Science Academy
Kensington and Chelsea

City of London KPMG Academy
Hackney

City of London Academy
Islington

The Corby City Academy
Northamptonshire

Excelsior
Newcastle

Falmer Academy
Brighton and Hove

Folkstone Academy
Kent

Grace Academy Coventry
Coventry

Harris Boys Academy East Dulwich
Southwark

Harris City Academy Crystal
Palace
Croydon

The Harris Academy South
Norwood
Croydon

Havelock Academy
North-east Lincolnshire

(Academy name to be confirmed)
Herefordshire

Hirst Academy
Northumberland

Hylton Red House Academy
Sunderland

Langley Academy
Slough

Leigh City Technology College
Kent

JCB Academy
Staffordshire

Kingshurst Academy
Solihull

Madeley Academy
Telford and Wrekin

Marsh
Kent

Merchant's Academy Withywood
Bristol

Milton Keynes
Milton Keynes

Montgomery
Kent

(Academy name to be confirmed)
Northamptonshire

North Oxfordshire Academy
Oxfordshire

(Academy name to be confirmed)
Nottingham

Oasis Academy, North-east
Lincolnshire 1
North-east Lincolnshire

Oasis Academy, North-east
Lincolnshire 2
North-east Lincolnshire

Oasis Academy
Bristol

Oasis Academy
Enfield

Pennywell Academy
Sunderland

The Pickering Academy
Kingston upon Hull

The Rhodesway Academy
Bradford

(Academy name to be confirmed)
Rochdale

St Mary Magdalene Academy
Islington

(Academy name to be confirmed)
Salford

The Samworth Academy
Leicester City

(Academy name to be confirmed)
Sandwell 2

(Academy name to be confirmed)
Sandwell 3

The Stadium Academy
Brent

Shakespeare Road
Lambeth

(Academy name to be confirmed)
Southwark

(Academy name to be confirmed)
Southwark

(Academy name to be confirmed)
South Gloucestershire

Sheppey
Kent

Skinners
Hackney

Stockport Academy
Stockport

The St Matthews Academy
Lewisham

Thomas Deason Academy
Peterborough

(Academy name to be confirmed)
Wandsworth

(Academy name to be confirmed)
Westminster

William Hulme's Academy
Manchester

Information from the DfES's Standards site, October 2006:
http://www.standards.dfes.gov.uk/academies/projects/development/

Index